Death Matters

HISTORY ✤ HUMOR ✤ ADVICE

Richard H. McHugh

HERITAGE BOOKS
2008

HERITAGE BOOKS

AN IMPRINT OF HERITAGE BOOKS, INC.

Books, CDs, and more—Worldwide

For our listing of thousands of titles see our website
at
www.HeritageBooks.com

Published 2008 by
HERITAGE BOOKS, INC.
Publishing Division
100 Railroad Ave. #104
Westminster, Maryland 21157

International Standard Book Numbers
Paperbound: 978-0-7884-4557-6
Clothbound: 978-0-7884-7174-2

Dedicated to the memory of my wife, Jinnie Robinson McHugh, who died July 16, 2007.
I miss her.

And to my children, who endured a great deal.

Also dedicated to my computer associate, Erin Pinkston, without whom this book would not have been completed.

A TRIBUTE FROM AN OLD FRIEND

It's been there forever, it seems to some

The funeral home on Old 41

A place we went in times of sorrow

To seek surcease for the morrow

Kindly hands to guide us through

Extended to all by Mr. McHugh

The grandfather first and then the son

Handed down to Richard, the final one

The building is there, the one we knew

But it's not the same, without McHugh

—Lorene Nell Davidson, age 91

CONTENTS

Chapter 1

Turn of the Century

To anyone who has studied sociology, economics, or any of the myriad of subjects concerned with man's relationship to man, Death Matters. Most of us learn that one difficult problem we face during our time on this earth is the death of anyone in our immediate family or a close friend. All deaths from this group hurt us deeply, but after a near lifetime working in the funeral business, I can assure you the loss of a child to parents, especially to a mother, is the most agonizing death experience for any of us.

We live our lives anticipating the death of grandparents, parents, perhaps a sibling, with always a 50% chance of losing our spouse. When we lose a child we lose a part of ourselves. Medical science has continually reduced the possibilities of the death of young children. In a way these advances make these death even more traumatic since they are so rare. Even tiny babies of less than two pounds have an excellent chance of surviving today. In the beginning of my career many children were taken by such diseases as scarlet fever, polio, whooping cough, measles, chicken pox, and strep throat.

*Marriage
License*

Partnership Agreement

Corporate Contract

Many of these diseases, once called the childhood diseases, are gone from the picture. Even many of the more deadly causes of death, such as some kinds of leukemia, flu, yellow fever, typhoid fever, bubonic plague can be fought if not conquered. Nature still finds new ways to end our lives sometimes through the mutation of bacteria and viruses or new deadly diseases such as Aids and Alzheimer's. Nature has always found new ways to end the lives of humans and always will. Aids and Alzheimer's are really fairly new in the scheme of things.

Death Matters have always included accidents. Falls, drowning, burns, and lightning have been with us throughout history. Mass killers such as earthquakes, tornadoes, floods, glaciers, and volcanoes have taken people in sometimes enormous numbers. Scientific advances outside medicine add to our deaths. Automobile and airplane accidents, industrial explosions, railroad crashes, and improvements to military weapons have all increased the death rate on a world-wide basis. We continually add to the ways we can get out of this world, and in more recent times we have begun to add to the ways we can get into it, through artificial birth methods such as cloning, fertilizing of the egg outside the body and several other innovative methods.

The other way that death affects our lives is through the changes of relationships that occur among us at the time of death. Many long term relationships cease. Marriage comes to mind first. but death also ends many business relationships such as partnerships. Corporations can also be changed forever by deaths of certain members. When a death comes about in many of these circumstances, people must be found with certain qualities to see that the activities and goals of the businesses do not have to change. Great amounts of money and other assets can change hands due to death. Life insurance, business agreements, professional contracts, retirement plans and medical plans are changed after long being considered etched in concrete. So a part of all our lives is affected by Death Matters in more ways than one. We must plan our business and professional relationships to take death in consideration just as we do our personal affairs since death is as certain to end these entities created by man just as surely as it ends the lives of the men who brought them into existence.

I think that is one of the things I would most like to make clear to my readers. Planning is the key to an acceptance of all of the effects of death. Death can come without warning, after long illness, by self design or murder, but you can be sure that it will come and change if not destroy our best laid personal or business plans or relationships. You can't win but, in certain ways, you can cut your losses.

The care and disposal of the dead has been part of the life of human beings much, much longer than almost any other activity man has performed from his beginning to the present. Some of the earliest men were called hunters and gatherers, but they also cared for the dead. We are going to spend quite a portion of our time together recalling the beginning of the care of the dead, its development, improvement, and growth into the multi-billion dollar vocation or profession into which it has evolved. The history of these changes and growth has been torturous, contentious and irregular. It has been involved with the history and development of many other forms of human activity, such as religion, science, social behavior, military practices, medical study and practice, education, and cultural mores to name a few. We will be seeing how all these and many other efforts have affected and been affected by caring for the dead. Problems arising from the care of the dead can be multiplied by the manner in which death occurred, by the number of deaths which have occurred, or by the place in which the death(s) happened, or a myriad of other situations. You have read of deaths meeting each or all of the complications that I am going to mention here, but let me point out how these things can add to the complexities of deaths. If the cause of death is from a disease that can be transmitted to survivors by contact with parts of the body of he deceased, those in charge of the care of disposing of the body must protect others. Thorough embalming, complete cleansing, disposal of clothing worn, all these things become more important. An accident involving tens or hundreds of victims puts those in charge with identification problems, storage of the remains during identification, and transportation to the place of service and burial chosen by the next of kin. The place of death comes into play when locations such as at the bottom of a mine, the top of a mountain, or within the confines of a ship that has been sunk. Obviously these examples could continue endlessly, but my point is that whoever is responsible for handling such arrangements must be prepared to handle them in a great, great number of dissimilar circumstances. Those in charge may be government officials, military officers, police officers, people in charge of conveyances involved in accidents, in addition to funeral directors.

Almost everyone thinks of death and disposal of the dead in terms of the last time they were involved in a funeral and burial. In many cases, this can be when they lost a grandparent forty years ago. Most of the funerals that the firm in charge of this last funeral of yours still find most of their services of that type. But when we think of the complications discussed above we realize that the firm that handled Grandma or Grandpa's service must be trained, experienced and equipped as far as possible to work in these more complicated happenings. One more thing has influenced these matters. As time has passed, the public has grown to expect firms involved in the funeral business to provide first class memorial services without regard to the many types of death and surrounding situations we have alluded to above.

At the outset, however, I want to describe how my family came to be involved in this field. My family was active in the funeral business from 1908 until 1985, or almost eighty years. Many other funeral businesses began earlier or lasted longer than ours, and many others grew into much, much larger organizations until, in fairly recent times, huge business organizations with hundreds of locations in all parts of this country as well as other nations, have changed the idea that long existed of privately owned and operated businesses that provided a very personal and necessary service to the families of a deceased person at a time of great need and, in small towns at least, usually on a one to one relationship.

Early in the twentieth century, my grandfather put himself, his family and its next two generations into this business of caring and disposing of the dead. He begin this process by moving his wife, two daughters and a son from west of the town of Prairie Creek, Indiana, to a home within the slightly larger town of Shelburn, Indiana. They left behind the remains of another son, buried in West Lawn Cemetery located between their home and the town of Prairie Creek. A small monument still can be found showing that the young boy was named Wilbur. He lies alone in a four-grave lot that will never be filled, since I went to the authorities of the cemetery a few years ago in an effort to return the unused burial spaces, but the cemetery did not accept returned burial spaces.

My grandfather had farmed with his father until he was old enough to have had a wife and the five children mentioned above. I have neither heard nor read of this portion of my grandfather's life, but I do know that early in the twentieth century he made a decision to make a major change in his life and the life of his wife, surviving children and the next two generations. There is no indication that this decision was made for financial considerations, since the farm provided income for my family until it was sold by my sister and I in 1991. Prior to leaving the farm my grandfather entered into an agreement with a nearby farmer to take over the operation of our family farm. This agreement, which was never put on paper and which was made without the advice of an attorney lasted for three generations on one side, and for four generations on the other. The farm was finally sold to the grandson of the farmer who started farming for my family. We did use an attorney at the time of the sale. I also know a little about the sale of the business, since I was the one who sold it.

So we know about when my grandfather left the farm. We know where he went, it appears we will never know the actual reason why, but we can picture how he moved. At this time in history you didn't call Mayflower or United and have them show up with an enormous truck and a series of boxes of all sizes in which to place all of your belongings, which were then transported to your new address and placed in the rooms you indicated on the boxes. You couldn't even call Two Men and a Truck, or Back Breaker Movers, as you might today if money were a little short and the trip wasn't too long.

In 1904 or 05 you took the family wagon, hitched up a pair of mules, loaded up everything you could afford to take and took off on your own. You might have sold some of the larger pieces of furniture to lighten the load on your back, or the wagon, or the mules. All of them had a limit. If you were fortunate enough to have a relative or friend with a wagon, two mules and a rare day off you might have gotten some help, and you could have used it. Roads were dirt; plans had to be made for water, food and rest. The trip to Shelburn was over twenty miles and would require an early start, good weather and cooperation of the mules to accomplish in one day. If you couldn't make it, you did it all over the next day. There was one great advantage for my father, he was deemed old enough to ride one of the mules.

The family arrived at their new home, which was a two-story white clapboard house in Shelburn and remained the home of my grandfather until about a week prior to his death some thirty years later. The family set up housekeeping, and my grandfather assumed his role as the provider. Everyone in Prairie Creek, as well as in Shelburn, were residents of Indiana and as such were entitled to the appellation of Hoosiers, and I think you are entitled to know the origin and explanation of this term, of which there are several. Pioneers floating down the Ohio River who saw bon fires along the north side of the river are said to have called, "Who's there?" Grain haulers from the area were asked when they arrived in New Orleans (which was a hell of a trip!) "Who's yours?" when asked to identify their flatboats; and folks who traveled from Indiana to southern cities were said to have been called Hoosiers as a term of derision, such as hillbillies. My particular favorite explanation for the term involves those people whose responsibility it was to clean up the taverns or drinking establishments after a particularly rough night and enquired "Who's ear?" when picking up such objects that had been lost by their rightful owners due to the bite of an antagonist or the use of his knife. Whatever, we have been Hoosiers for a long, long time! Very few states can claim a more unique name.

I want to mention one other item from the family history on the farm. My father told how everyone placed a large boulder on their harrow (an implement used to break up plowed ground), which was to be pulled by a horse or mule in accomplishing the work with the driver, in this case, my father walking behind. After a couple of days of this, he threw the boulder from the harrow, tied on a kitchen chair and rode the chair rather than walking behind. He was chastised for this as being lazy rather than being praised for being innovative in labor saving ideas. This also indicates that my family continued to work at the farm on occasion after the move, since he would have been too young to operate the harrow before the move from the farm. Helping out continued during planting and harvesting seasons for many years. I was even a part of it during my teens, driving a tractor to pull hay to the barn. I can still remember the size and variety of the meals served at noontime.

It seems while all of the men and older boys were engaged in the day's farm work, all of the ladies and older girls spent the morning and afternoon preparing meals for everyone. Since all hands worked hard all day, three enormous meals were an important part of every day. I wasn't used to this, but I did pretty much my share due to the amount of work they were getting out of me.

I have been unable to learn my grandfather's reason to move to Shelburn. Although he might have had another job of some nature first, it was not long before he was in the livery business, in which the operator rented horses, mules, and buggies or wagons to persons in need of such equipment for long or short periods of time. Almost every town had a livery stable, and had he known Shelburn did not have one might have been the reason for the move. The business was successful since an early photo of the street where it was located shows a good-sized building with the inscription Livery Stable painted on the side. My grandfather had a partner by the name of Harry Wilson in this endeavor. As time went by, they discovered that they were increasingly renting horses and buggies, (called rigs) to people for the purpose of attending funerals. This led, rather naturally, to lining up the rigs for funerals at the residence of the deceased or at a church being used for the purpose. This service led them to being a part of many funeral services.

In most small towns at this time there was no one in charge of a funeral service. Usually an Aunt Grace or Grandma Wilma saw to the arrangements. Someone had to notify relatives and friends of the family who had suffered the loss. Many times a minister needed to be made aware of the situation. Everyone needed to know of the time and place of a planned service and when the family was accepting guests to express their condolences. Friends had to be advised as to the location of burial space in the family or church cemetery that was to be opened for the interment. This onerous task was performed free gratis by friends of the family, although a meal was usually provided at the conclusion of the service for all who had assisted the family in any way. The mentioning of opening the grave reminds me of an occasion when I assisted in the task. Once a family insisted we had opened the wrong grave on their family plot. Although my father always felt we had not made a mistake, I immediately offered to go home, change clothes and help open the new grave and close the one we were not going to use.

When I got back on the scene, I grabbed the spade, jumped into the partially completed grave and proceeded to break the spade in two at my first effort. I hadn't given the real grave openers time to advise me that the spade handle was cracked and you had to push the blade forward prior to lifting the load from the grave. It took several hours to locate another spade and the job was not completed until dark.

Let's get back to Aunt Grace and Grandma Wilma, as they worked toward completing the arrangements. If the deceased were a man, they probably sought the assistance of another relative or two of that gender to help with the bathing of the remains of the deceased, dressing them in their best clothes or perhaps in a robe and slippers. When all had been done that could be done, the remains, male or female were placed on a cot or perhaps on a door, either of which was supplied with a pillow and covered with material of some sort. Black crepe paper or other material was used to cover mirrors and surround windows in an effort to prevent anyone form viewing the soul escaping the body. The period provided for friends and relatives to call on the family was referred to as the wake, as it is still called in many areas, although it is called a visitation now around here. A wake was intended to give all involved assurance that the deceased was really gone and not in some form of coma. In the absence of embalming there was no guarantee that the death had occurred, and almost everyone was familiar with an occasion when evidence of life appeared after several hours or even a day or two. I have seen early casket advertisements which showed a contrivance that allowed a string or ring to be placed on the finger of the deceased and attached to a bell above ground that would ring in the event of movement. There was a widespread and sincere horror of being buried alive.

The wake varied in length at the request of the family. Weather was one consideration, with hot weather holding such affairs to a lesser period. The wake was almost always overnight, and many friends and nearly all relatives remaining for the whole time. So you might have one day and night or two days and one night or even longer. One of the main features of the wake was the quality and quantity of the food. There were at least three large tables, all overladen. One was for meat dishes, one for fruits and vegetables, and the last smothered with pies, cakes, cobblers, cookies and every other known dessert. Every lady attending the wake outdid herself with the preparation, and all the guests ate for most of the period of the wake. There were other practices that have ended with time and the almost universal use of embalming. The use of pennies to close the eyes and the use of a cloth to hold the jaw up were universal. In some instances the solemn occasion became a little more boisterous than good taste would suggest. As we mentioned the wake lasted all night, with the ladies singing hymns and burning candles and the men describing the good qualities of the lost friend or relative, and perhaps sampling the liquid refreshments such as home brew, white lightning, or even some store-bought libation.

The wake served the function of providing a meeting of friends, neighbors and relatives. It allowed a period of time for more distant people to arrive, and provided everyone with an opportunity to reminisce about their friend or relative. Usually the good qualities of the deceased were covered in more depth than any frailties. It has long been said "the evil a man does dies with him, the good lives on." Everyone present could tell at least one story benefiting the reputation of the departed. It was not the time to discuss his shortcomings.

I have covered many but not all of the required duties and responsibilities that need to be taken care of at the time of any death. An accident, a murder, a suicide or a death by communicable disease brought more detailed requirements. In the case of a communicable disease, for instance, early disposal of the remains was necessary to prevent a potential epidemic. These diseases included measles, small pox, whooping cough and scarlet fever along with the more serious such as cholera or flu. Children were particularly susceptible to the epidemics Accidents, murders, and suicides all drew more attention, and everyone was interested in the particulars of any death(s) of this nature.

Due to the interest in multiple deaths or deaths of other than normal causes, local and state governments and the press were all becoming interested in deaths and their causes. These deaths provided information that was needed to be retained for medical history and for criminal records. Soon it was required by the State government that a Certificate of Death be filed in each county. The certificate had to be signed by a medical doctor or a health department official if no doctor was in attendance. If there was an indication of an accident, suicide or murder the county coroner signed the certificate after an investigation. The press was interested in the news value of all deaths and soon carried personal information and time and place of deaths, along with major stories about accidents, multiple deaths, and murders. Thus began the obituary column or page. Reporters were assigned to the death of prominent people or to the more unusual deaths we described above.

In view of all of the above would you not agree that some official, administrator, busybody, or director, that's it, a funeral director, who took care of all those details, was desperately needed by the community in which a deceased resident lived, as well as by his or her family? And thus was a new vocation born in almost all cities and towns. In the case of Shelburn, my grandfather assumed these responsibilities in addition to lining up the rigs, and he began to charge for his time, service, and knowledge. This became the lot of a high percentage of livery business operators. In many cases these beginnings of funeral businesses continued from generation to generation, and formed many of the firms that exist today.

There was another form of business that also was the source of many funeral businesses. The cabinet or furniture maker, who also was in business in most small communities, began to construct a coffin for a deceased person as the need arose. Over a period of years he began to keep a supply offering a choice to families who had suffered a loss. The rates of death were high among all age groups, and the need was broadened by the number of children who were lost due to lack of medical knowledge, poor diet, and hard work. Many furniture makers turned from making coffins to selling them and thus entered the funeral business by a different route. Some also became casket-manufacturing companies and grew into sizable firms, the largest in the world being Batesville Casket Company, located in Batesville, Indiana as a part of Hillenbrand Industries.

I can remember my father telling me that in the 1920s they carried caskets of every foot in length from one and one-half feet to adult sizes in order to provide whatever size might be needed. By the time of my tenure, we only carried stillborn size for children, since death did not claim children of other ages very often. Also, casket manufacturers could supply you with whatever size was needed in a matter of hours. Accidents soon became the leading cause of death for children as medical science found cures for the diseases that had earlier taken many of them.

It was not an easy task, even with a new Funeral Director in town, to conduct a funeral in a residence, although it was a practice that was continued for a long, long time in the area in which we served. A church was better for a funeral, but not all families had church relationships. In addition, many churches were constructed for a church sized crowd and on many occasions funeral crowds exceeded church crowds. I'm not commenting on religious practices in our society here, I'm just stating the facts as I saw them develop.

There were many services the new funeral director could provide if he could have his own business place. Let's review them. A table on which the remains could be bathed and dressed and also used for embalming which we will discuss in detail later, a room with a display of caskets, burial clothing such as robes and slippers and later gowns and suits, an office where arrangements for the visitation and service could be made and where records and correspondence could be handled, a room where funeral services could be held (many times by moving caskets and office equipment), a moveable device upon which the casket could be placed with proper lighting, folding chairs and furniture, and space for relatives and friends to gather if the wake was to be held at this location. Later stands for flowers, a register book for visitors to sign, thank you cards for flowers received and other services performed were all supplied. Most funeral homes had a drive where rigs and automobiles could be lined up, a hearse to be drawn by a matched team of horses at the front, until all of these vehicles were replaced by motorized units. In many businesses a sign was placed outside showing the name and time and place of visitation and service for those whose death had occurred. Services provided by the Funeral Director included notifying relatives and friends, inserting a notice in the newspaper if one was available, collecting the information for the required death certificate and securing the signature of the doctor in attendance and filing the form with the Board of Health, from which a Burial-Transit permit would be issued, notifying the minister chosen by the family, along with musicians desired, getting in contact with those who were to open and close the burial space, ordering flowers for the family if requested, and reserving time at the church if one was to be used. Many firms used a form to check off all the items at the time each was completed. I used to think I could keep in mind all of the details of three funerals without writing anything down. That was important because forgetting anything listed above could lose a lot of good will with the family.

It was my observation that you were working for a family at a time when it was easy to do so. People wanted Mom's funeral to be just right, and if you were doing your best they would understand and forgive minor omissions. The funeral industry received a lot of criticism from the press and other pundits that advantage was taken of people at the time of the loss of a loved one by selling merchandise or services priced above their need or ability to pay. I am sure that this occurred, as it is the essence of capitalism, but I was aware of few, if any, firms near me that could be accused of such practices. The firms that made up our competition and the firms that I did business with throughout the Midwest were reputable and dealt fairly with the public. Most of them were active in community affairs where they served and supported those affairs financially. Even in a practice as small as ours you dealt over the years with businesses throughout the country. We were always members of the National Funeral Directors Association, and if we had a call in California or Texas or Florida we selected a member of this organization from the list of members there and we were almost always pleased with the service and the prices.

I spoke at one funeral in my career. It was for a lovely lady who had lost her husband in a coal mining accident in the 1930s when I was a small boy. She was left with a number of children at a time when most ladies in this situation had very few choices of making a living. Taking in washing and domestic work were about the only choices for a quality person in the mold of this lady. There was no social security, no workmen's compensation, no union benefits, no company benefits, but lots of rent, food requirements, clothing, and school costs. Someone recommended her to my father and thus began a long and loving relationship between she and my family. She was the first of a number of ladies who served us in the funeral home. Many years later at her death her family related to me that she had always requested that I officiate at her funeral. I was flabbergasted, unqualified, scared and speechless. After remembering how much she had done for my family for so many years, I told them I would do as she had requested with two reservations. One, they were never to tell anyone not at the funeral I had done it, and second that I would receive nothing for my effort. I got through the service somehow, no one ever mentioned it to me again, but the family brought me a gold desk set inscribed with their thanks, which I certainly could not refuse.

Over the years you would be surprised how many families would inquire as to what they should do if they or a relative of theirs needed the services of a funeral director where they were living or traveling in a distant state. I always told them they were off to the right start by talking with someone they knew. I felt there was one controlling factor in a decision of this nature. If they wished a visitation or a funeral service in the distant area, then they should contact the funeral director where they were, select the merchandise, and have the remains shipped to us upon conclusion of the service there. They could also let us know what was needed when we received the remains. In most cases we would have a continued service and handle the burial arrangements. Things could be simplified and normally less expensive by contacting us direct, and having us contact the funeral home where they were located. This made the contact there wholesale. We would have preparation done by the funeral home there, with the body dressed and shipped to us in what was called a shipping container. We would pay the services of the distant firm and the transportation costs. The family would contact us upon their arrival home, purchase the funeral plus the charges we had paid and minus the cost of the work done by the firm where the death had occurred. We normally paid for the services at the other location and added the amount to our cash advance items. The services paid for at the other end were also deducted from our total. In such cases visitation and funeral were at our end where burial was final. I feel that I should mention that I have been out of the business for over twenty years and cremation and other factors, such as private planes and restricted service funerals have enhanced the arrangements I have described. There are now companies that will ship your remains into space or see that they are disposed of at the bottom of the sea. Freezing of the remains is available, so that the body can be brought back to normal temperature and take advantage of any cure that might have been developed for the cause of their death.

I remember a case which we called a "ship in" that occurred in 1956, that had an unusual twist. We received notice that we were to meet a train carrying he remains of a lady who had passed away in Minnesota. I remember the incident since we had recently purchased a 1956 hearse-ambulance combination that had a black body with a white top. This in itself was an occasion, since it was the first funeral coach in the area that was not all black in color. My father and I, rather proudly, drove the new vehicle to the train station, parked it on the downtown side of the building so everyone could see it and rather close to the track so we could load directly from the train to the hearse. We soon heard the train in the distance. At that time, trains did not have to slow for Shelburn, and it must have been going seventy-five miles an hour with the whistle screaming. It soon became evident that there would be no stopping in Shelburn. My father and I were standing not over ten feet from the track, more or less petrified as the train roared toward us. My father said, when it was about 100 feet from our site, "I don't think it's going to stop!" It couldn't have stopped in a mile. We learned later by phone inquiry that there had been a layover and two-hour delay in Chicago. The husband had left the train, had a few libations and not gotten back in time to see that his wife's body was transferred to the train we were meeting. He and his wife's remains arrived on the next train, but we didn't park as close to the tracks this time.

My father had one other experience at the train depot before it passed into history. He received word that a death had occurred at the depot area. This was in the middle of the night, and when he arrived there, the only light he saw was in a small shack located across the tracks. He walked over there and stepped in, where he saw five men arranged around a small table playing poker. He told them he was sorry to have bothered them but that he had received a call that there had been a death in the area. One of the players said, "O Yeah, we called you, Joe died a while back!" Joe was slumped over the table and the game was still in progress. Everyone has to have priorities. I also had an experience of this nature, someone called that a lady in town had died at her residence. When I arrived there, I found a young couple doing what was called "sparking" on the front porch. I apologized to the couple, knocked on the door and the lady who was supposed to be dead soon opened it. A jealous boyfriend had called me with some false information about her death. Everyone enjoyed pulling a prank on the local funeral director-ambulance provider. It was not unusual during Halloween time to get a call for an ambulance service in the country. Many times you would have to remove a barrier of trash, weeds and anything else that could be used to stop you. After picking up the patient (if there really was one), you would be forced to clear the road on your way back to town. This was supposed to be funny, but I can remember it having some serious consequences a few times.

Chapter 2

The Beginning of a Family Business

And so we have placed my grandfather as an early funeral director serving in the care of the dead with his partner from the former livery stable. I have to report a slight discrepancy at this point. While my grandfather's business records begin in 1908, they show no record of another owner. Once near the end of my career, I had a lady bring me a church fan, which was a typical advertising item in those days before air conditioning. Printed on the fan was the inscription, McHugh and Wilson, Funeral Directors. At the bottom was a date, 1911. I have been unable to account for this; perhaps Mr. Wilson was an employee whose name was used in the firm. I do remember being told that he was bought out or forced out very early in the history of the firm. I remember being made aware that there were some hard feelings so forced out seems to be most likely.

This leaves my grandfather as the sole owner and operator of McHugh Funeral Home, Shelburn, Indiana, with a wife, two daughters and a son. He operated the business in a building not too far from the livery stable and later moved to a more suitable building about two blocks west and across the railroad track, where it remained for quite a number of years. I remember this second building since the funeral home was located there until after I was in school. It was barely adequate with a small business office just inside the door with a casket selection room, embalming room, and storage rooms making up the rest of the building. I also remember there was a truck-sized door at the rear of the building where we brought in caskets which were shipped in pine boxes which were later used as outside containers for caskets in most burials until burial vaults came upon the scene several years after we were gone from this location. We left this location when the new brick funeral home was completed in 1936. This building remains in service today.

After we moved into the building that is briefly described above that my grandfather and father built for their office in Shelburn, my grandfather (not the funeral director, the other one) and I tore down the former funeral location I described above. This was a major job for a young boy of about 9 or 10 and his grandfather, but we managed to bring down the building with some professional help with the demolition. We managed to clean the brick and transport them to the location of the new building, where they were used to construct a 4-car garage next to the new funeral home which served the business for so many years. It is possible that you are not familiar with the term "cleaning brick" in this day of tearing down everything in the way of new construction and burying it or otherwise disposing of it. Cleaning brick is from another era when the remains of structures being town down were saved in so far as practical. Nails were removed from floor joists and wall studs, so that they could be used in other construction.

Bricks were cleaned, which meant that the old mortar was removed from the brick that fell or were removed from the walls of the building. It was not an easy task. You used a hammer and a hatchet or a hammer and a chisel and chopped away the old mortar. The bricks were then moved to the new building site.

Prior to building the new garage, I remember my father and I driving the hearse/ambulance to the downtown building each night for storage. We walked back to the funeral home and usually stopped at a small restaurant walking back to the new funeral home. Sometimes this was fairly late at night and we got into some pretty adult conversations with others on their way home from the tavern or where ever they had been. It was pretty heady stuff for a boy of my age, and I learned a few new words for my vocabulary. It was also a lot of fun, and I remember most of the people who participated, but died long ago.

Shelburn was founded by a man named Pascal Shelburn. He donated the land for the Shelburn Baptist Church and the East Ward School and laid out the town on each side of the railroad track, which ran through the center of the business district. There were advantages and disadvantages to the arrangement. For many years an interurban track was located just west of the railroad and the station for the interurban is still in its original location. An interurban was a rail line similar to a streetcar in that it received electric power from an overhead wire. It ran rather like a subway when it leaves the underground at the edge of a city serving communities just outside the city, but an interurban might run for a hundred miles or so. Subsequent to the closing of the interurban line, the station served as a temporary American Legion Post and later as a restaurant, although it has been vacant for many years. The railroad divided Shelburn almost equally in two areas, with an elementary school about five blocks east and west of the downtown. There were five crossings of the railroad, three of which had only crossing markers, with no flashing lights or guardrails. This led to an inordinate number of car and pedestrian train accidents over the years. Shelburn has also had some very tragic fires during its history. The most famous train accident was in the 1920s, when a main line passenger train jumped the track in the center of town. Fires in Shelburn include a three-house blaze on the main street three blocks west of downtown, .Three business buildings burned just east of the railroad in the center of the town, which were fortunately rebuilt soon after the blaze, this was in about 1939. Shelburn's main and one of its few industries burned on the west side of the tracks in a major catastrophe that ended the operation of a large portion of the company, although part of the business still exists under its second ownership since this fire. On one occasion we were having a normal funeral service in the Shelburn chapel. Much to our surprise and regret we learned that the feed store just across the street was burning, with smoke and flames bursting out of the upright or elevator part of the business. We decided to allow the funeral to continue, since it was nearly over. We placed an extension ladder against one side of the funeral home, soaked some old throw rugs and took them up to the two story roof and also managed to get some garden hose and extensions so that we could take the hose to the roof. Although some of the attendees at the funeral were aware that something unusual was going on, we felt we had the situation well in hand and no one was in immediate danger. Out of the blue, and not checking with us, the town marshal, of all people, stormed into the back of the chapel and shouted at the top of his considerable voice, "This building is on fire, everyone leave this building immediately!" You cannot imagine the uproar and confusion this announcement produced! Everyone went everyway! There was no stopping them! We finally got the casket into the hearse and the family into their cars and took the procession through the yard on the opposite side of the funeral home from the feed store/elevator. Neither our funeral home nor any of the occupants was ever in any danger, but someone could have easily been hurt in the melee following the exclamation from the town marshal. I told him what I thought of his actions after returning from the cemetery. What a way for an official to act!

Until the middle 1930s, U.S. 41 made four turns through the town. The road was single lane, and that led to a lot of automobile accidents. I remember not too proudly one in which a man and his wife had a single vehicle accident on the turn just north of town. My father and I were wearing work clothes and engaged in an outdoor project, although it was quite cool. Neither of us had any money on us. We got into the ambulance, which had seen better years and headed for the site. The man requested that we take his wife, who was the more seriously injured to a Terre Haute hospital, which was about twenty miles north on U.S. 41. The man complained all the way that they were freezing in the back of the ambulance, while my father and I were plenty warm. I was driving and checked everything over several times but could not discover anything wrong, explaining they were probably cold from being exposed at the accident scene. When we reached about ten or twelve blocks from the hospital, the ambulance ran out of gasoline and died in the middle of the street. We called a nearby funeral home for another ambulance, transferred the patient and traded our cot for theirs, after telling them we would trade back a day or two later. After the patient had been moved in a warm ambulance to the hospital, my father and I called a service station a few blocks away and asked them to bring us a container of gasoline. We followed them to their location, ordered the tank filled, and authorized a quart of oil to be added upon their checking the oil level. Upon completion of these services, my father asked to see the credit department. He was quickly told they had none, but he told them they were going to have to open one since we had no money. I stopped there the next day to pay them off, but we sure didn't have enough nerve to send a statement for the ambulance service. We did offer to pay the other funeral home for picking up our patient, but they said the folks had paid them for their trip and used some choice words about our service. By the way, there was a lever you had to switch to transfer heat to the rear of the ambulance; it had not been moved so they were right about the lack of heat in the backend!

I remember another event that happened when we picked up an ambulance we had in for repairs at a garage where the foreman was a friend of ours. He said he had a driver who would take my father home since we had gone in two cars. He took him home all right at speeds of over a hundred miles an hour, which was the highest speed the ambulance ever attained. The ambulance portion of our business is coming up later with some serious as well as some more forgettable runs in my memory.

The population of Shelburn has fallen since the beginning of the operation of the funeral home almost a hundred years ago.

The town peaked in population in the 1920s at about 2500. It is also said of those times that you could hear seven mine whistles each morning and evening from the mines surrounding the town. It is also reported that there were seven churches in the community as well as seven saloons. As of this writing there are zero mines, two drinking establishments and five churches, and a population of about twelve hundred. There is still evidence of the mines around the town in each direction. Some areas devoid of plant growth, large piles of gob (waste earth that came up with coal) or abandoned buildings or equipment mark these locations. A few of the mines had small residential areas around them. The largest of these communities was south of a mine called Jackson Hill, and not surprisingly the community was also called Jackson Hill. At one time there were about 275 residents living here. There was a store located in the community, offering necessities and a few of the luxuries of life as they were defined at that time. Jackson Hill was located in the next township south of Shelburn and the children from there attended the high school in the County Seat, Sullivan, which served the children of that township. It is worth mentioning that Jackson Hill supplied many fine athletes in all sports. There were several all state football players and one next generation basketball player who played professional basketball for the Los Angeles Lakers.

Many of the miners came directly to Shelburn after emigrating from parts of Europe, particularly Poland and the Balkan and Baltic states. Some of the wives came with their husbands while others were sent for later after funds could be accumulated for the trip. Many of these ladies lived the rest of their lives in Jackson Hill and many never learned English. Their children and grandchildren of course fit right in with the new world life. Jackson Hill was a place where the fortunes of the coal industry controlled the lives of the inhabitants. There was either a drop in demand for the coal or a strike every spring or both. Miners who got behind with their debts at the company store were paid in script, which could only be spent there, and a famous singer, Tennessee Ernie Ford wrote a song about their plight, entitled "Sixteen Tons." One line went, "you load sixteen tons and what do you get, another day older and deeper in debt." Seldom has a song got to the center of a way of life more accurately or more expressively than this one.

We, of course, provided funeral and ambulance service to the Jackson Hill community. These folks were a pleasure to work with, appreciative and always paid their debts. Many of them were of the Catholic Faith, and I can remember my father saying he never had a Catholic dollar on his books.

Jackson Hill was one of the focal points of the effort of the United Mine Workers under John L. Lewis to unionize the mining industry in our area in the 1930s. I can remember, as a child, seeing the camp fires of the State Militia just south of State Highway 48 which ran from Shelburn to Hymera, a town you will learn to know from my family locating its second funeral home there. These unionization efforts caused a number of physical confrontations between the miners and strike-breakers in the employment of the companies. There were even some fatalities. When my oldest son was in college, he wrote a paper regarding these times and told of his interviews with the participants. Even forty years later, some of these men would not discuss the events, while others told where they were positioned and who was the target of the shooting. My father told of often driving the ambulance down the road to the mine after injured workers. The Militia and strikebreakers would be on one side of the road and the union organizers and the miners on the other. He said he entered and left the mine area as quickly as possible and his eyes never left the road to either side.

The work which my grandfather chose as a means of advancement for his family and those who came after his is what came to be called the funeral business and it has a history that we are going to cover to begin to understand how it came to be what we know it as today.

Chapter 3

A Much, Much Earlier Time

By far the most famous country in the history of the world in terms of caring for the dead is Egypt. Their reputation is so far ahead of anyone else, that such a comparison is about the same as comparing a candle to the sun. This is not completely true, but books, movies, and television have convinced us that Egypt was the frontrunner. Remember the traveling display of King Tutankhamen and his treasures that covered the United States not too many years ago. We were all overcome by it, and there are probably 1000 persons who are familiar with the name Tutankhamen for everyone who can name any other mummy, although not many who can spell it. The Egyptians were not really that far ahead of many other civilizations in the two parts of serving the dead as we are going to see, but they have held the title of leaders ever since they started it. The two parts of this care are embalming and mummification. They came about for reasons of religion and public health. The religion of the Egyptians promised life after death. Embalming and mummification were an effort to allow those living in the next world to do so in the same body as the one in which they lived in this one. While they could never point to anyone who had reached this success, they continued to try probably because this second world was expected to be at least two thousand years in the future. I don't believe I need to explain the needs of public health quite so completely, since if nothing had been done with the dead public health would have soon brought itself to attention in an emphatic way. Embalming and mummification took away this problem.

I am sorry to have to report that embalming in Egypt was practiced along with another ancient human practice, that of class distinction, which is still in our culture. Three levels of embalming technique existed. The first was for the Pharaohs (or Kings), for high government officials, and for the extremely wealthy. In this technique, the internal organs (viscera) were removed from the body cavities (thoracic and abdominal), and the head or cranium. Everything was deposited in separate ritualistic containers called "canopic jars," which were filled with a local natural (salt) solution called natron. The body cavities were then dried and filled with spices, herbs and bitumen and then sewed closed. At this point the entire body was immersed in the natron solution for up to forty days, after which the body was straightened and composed, completing the embalming process. The body was then mummified by wrapping it in hundreds of yards of linen bandages soaked in cedar or perhaps juniper oils. Between the layers of cloth herbs and spices and valuable ornaments were sometimes placed. Gum Arabic covered each layer of cloth, hermetically sealing the remains from the atmosphere. The body was then placed in a wooden or stone sarcophagus before being entombed, which we must also consider after discussing the embalming of the other two levels of Egyptian citizenry.

Before continuing we should mention that some authorities mention special attention and care of the heart, which was considered the center of life.

The middle ranking Egyptians were embalmed by making an incision into the right side of the trunk, where corrosive materials were place inside to dissolve the internal organs, the body was then placed in the natron solution for up to 40 days and then, completely dehydrated, was filled with resins, sewed closed and the remains returned to the family with or without mummification.

The remaining class of Egyptians, which amounted to about eighty percent of the total population, was merely immersed in natron or sometimes bitumen and then mummified in a less complex manner. It has been estimated that about seventy million mummies were created in the long period of Egyptian history.

To continue with the care of the remains of the upper echelons of Egyptian society, entombment was varied, unbelievably expensive in some cases, and had some interesting sidelights. Following the embalming and mummification of the earthly remains of the kings and the very wealthy, the remains are thought to have been shipped by way of the Nile River on funerary ships to the site of the pyramids provided for those with enough power or wealth to be entitled to the use of such edifices. Only slightly over 100 pyramids have been discovered, although the remains of others made of less substantial materials have been found near the great pyramids. When related to the estimate of seventy million mummies we can see that only a miniscule number of the dead were deemed deserving of this honor. The others were buried in caves in the mountain rocks, in smaller tombs at the pyramid sites, or in rock hollows below their homes, or in the desert, or in plain earth burial spaces. We should also note that the pyramids did not stand alone. They were a part of groups of buildings, such as temples, chapels, other tombs, or massive walls. In the beginning of the pyramid era about 3000 B.C., an architect called Imbotey built a rudimentary pyramid for King Dyoser. This was the origin of the pyramid era. He built the first one by placing six bench-shaped mounds called mastabas, which had previously been tombs of the great, on top of each other. Since the mastabas were of different sizes they formed a step pyramid. They contained passageways and a burial chamber for the king. Almost all of the pyramids were paid for by the person to be buried there or by his family, although the cost usually came from the people in some way, another tradition that continues to this day, when the rich and famous find methods to pass their greatest expenses on to someone else through many innovative ways.

The Great Pyramid at Giza, constructed for the burial of King Snufur by his son, King Khufu, covered thirteen acres of desert. The sides, which rose at an angle of 51 degrees 52 minutes, were over 755 feet long. The pyramid was 481 feet high and the stones used in its construction were estimated to weigh from over two tons to fifteen tons each.

It has long been a mystery as to how the Great Pyramid was built. Egyptian workers were supplied with copper tools, such as chisels, drills and saws that might have been able to cut the stones. It is considered probable they were dragged up ramps built around the Pyramids, which were removed when it was completed. An abrasive powder such as sand might have been used with the drills and saws in the cutting of the great blocks of stone. It is even more difficult to understand how the granite used in the passageways and burial chambers had been cut and formed, although an abrasive material would have certainly been required.

Pyramids from the Fifth and Sixth Dynasties had inscriptions carved in them revealing information regarding the Egyptian religion in the form of picture writing called hieroglyphics. Some of the hieroglyphics also told stories of the King buried within. The Greek historian, Herodius, estimated in the fifth century, B.C. that 100,000 men worked parts of twenty years to complete the Great Pyramid. Later estimates are much lower. Regardless of the number of workers or the time actually spent, the building of the Great Pyramid remains one of the most compelling mysteries and accomplishments of ancient history.

While the Egyptians were the super heroes of early embalming and mummification, they were not alone in their efforts. Many other civilizations in other parts of the world were involved in their forms of these practices. Quick drying was the most common method to accomplish mummification. Since neither bacteria nor fungi can grow in the absence of water, drying in the sun, or with smoke, fire or chemicals can make mummies. Freezing works since neither the bacteria or fungi that cause mortification survive freezing. The burial of a body in a peat bog has produced mummification, so the process can be brought about by many circumstances and is sometimes in the form of an accident.

When mankind attempted to bring about mummification purposefully, they turned to some form of embalming, as we have discussed in regard to Egypt and its religion. Many other early religions and some that still exist have believed in similar fashion that the body must be preserved for a long period of time to give the deceased an opportunity to exist in the distant future promised by their religion in the same body they had occupied during their worldly existence.

Thus different forms of embalming and mummification were discovered and developed in widely separated countries throughout the world. The Chinchoros in Chile, and the Incas in the Andes Mountains in Peru, where the practices were highly developed particularly for those killed in religious sacrifice, are two examples.

In New Guinea, the dead were smoke-cured, covered with a protective layer of clay and propped up in scaffolds overlooking their village. The Aleut people, who lived in the Aleutian Islands off the coast of Alaska, mummified their dead by removing the internal organs and stuffing the cavities of the body with dry grass. The body was laid in a stream, where the rushing water dissolved the body's fat and washed it away leaving only muscle and skin, which were allowed to dry. The mummy produced by this method was wrapped in layers of waterproof leather and woven clothing and placed in a warm cave.

In 1991, a mummy was found in a glacier near the Austrian-Italian border, where it was proved by radiocarbon dating to have been since 3350 to 3300 B.C. He was carrying a bow and arrows and had grass stuffed into his shoes. The state of preservation was remarkable. Hunters found the best- preserved human remains in North America in Greenland, where the body of a baby, a young boy and six women were located in a shallow cave protected by an over-hanging rock. They had been there for about five hundred years. Preservation in each of these cases was remarkable, some through mummification and others by nature.

I have saved one other rather prevalent burial custom in many of these societies for last. Very frequently the possessions of the deceased, called burial goods, were placed with the body in whatever was the final resting place of the deceased. These objects might include favorite jewelry, clothing, tools or keepsakes. Remember, teachings led to the belief that such objects would be desired or needed in the next life. Some religions even led in some cultures to the sacrificing of slaves, workers and in some cases wives, children and family members, so they could be interred with the important devoted leader and serve him in his after life.

In many cultures and countries of the Far East, practices similar to those described above were common. In China, India, Indonesia, and other countries burial goods and in many cases living workers and slaves were included. In the Hindu religion, wives were expected to throw their living body onto the funeral pyre of their husband, which was usually floating on a raft on a sacred river. China was famous for the use of terra cotta representations of soldiers and slaves for this practice, but wives and other members of a great man's household were often included.

The wide distribution of the practices of embalming and mummification and the ways they were performed throughout many portions of the world stress the need for these practices, which we have pointed out are religion and public health. Geographic factors sometimes led to variations in the procedures, such as extreme altitude or heat.

The disappearance of the pyramids is of almost as much interest as their construction. The enormous expense hastened the ending of the construction era. The pyramids were built in an area of the globe with extremely hot sun and a great deal of blowing sand that also led to their destruction. Another factor was the continuing robbing of the pyramids of the mummies and the burial goods we have described. Regardless of the subterranean tunnels and the huge boulders placed at the entrance of the burial chambers, robbers never gave up and were successful enough to discourage the construction. The successful robbing of a grave could make a robber wealthy for life, and the practice remained until fairly recent times. The amazing discovery and saving of the mummy of King Tutankhamen and the treasures from his burial chamber did not occur until well into the twentieth century.

The Roman Empire was one of the greatest civilizations of ancient history. For its time it developed the greatest culture, the most advanced form of government, the greatest military forces and the most effective and efficient control over the citizenry yet to come into existence. It also advanced the care and burial of its citizens recognizing that as a reflection on their way of life. Through relics that have survived, through great written histories and entertainment extravaganzas that are still being produced, we are well blessed with descriptions of the Roman way of life. Who has not been exposed to books, movies or television tributes to the Roman Empire? It is difficult to limit our interest to the care of the dead. All of the studies and presentations mentioned above tempt us to more glorious fields. Oh Well! The customs of death and burial were also embellished in their own way.

Death in Rome was accepted as a part of life. An early example of great loss of life that has been studied for many years is the eruption of Vesuvius in 70 A.D. The victims of Vesuvius were mostly burned to ashes in the eruption or were covered with ash until their remains decomposed, so that those interested could make plaster casts of the space occupied to discover the horror of their death, and little identification was possible.

Crucifixion was a method used in Rome to execute enemies of the state. The most important death of this nature was that of Jesus Christ. Many of his followers were crucified upside down. The other form of death that the Romans made world famous was the fights to the death in the Colosseum and other arenas throughout the empire. Mass deaths for entertainment included battles between animals and animals, animals and man, and most thrilling between man and man, and they amaze us to this day. Some of the cultures we have already covered inflicted deaths of this nature but not in an inspiring edifice built for this purpose and with a charge for admission.

So we'll start with the disposal of the dead in the Roman Colosseum as representative of such events. In animals versus animals and animals versus man, the victors usually consumed the conquered. It was in man versus man where death became heroic. These gladiators were selected many times from slaves captured in wars, returned to Rome where they were trained for years and finally entered the arena in fights for their lives. In many cases the crowd or the government official who was presenting the games decided the fate of the loser of these matches. This scene of the man in charge of the games asking the crowd for its vote on the life or death of the gladiator and then his final decision made for some of the most dramatic scenes in literature or great movies.

When a Roman of stature died, his family gathered to mourn the passing, calling the name of the deceased, wailing, and expressing their loss through actions against their bodies, although women were forbidden to scratch their face until bleeding occurred. To mark the event of the death of a Roman, cypress decked the front door of the residence, showing that the home was unclean. The body was washed, dressed in its best clothing, and quite often mummified. This was not done in imitation of Egyptian practices, but rather in the interest of the other cause of care, public health. Many Roman services and burials could last for a week and in summers Rome could be hot enough to require mummification. Also in Rome is the first mention of an actual person who cared for the death as a vocation. An undertaker, or libitianium, was often paid for performing the required services. The body, thus prepared, was placed in the atrium of the home, the feet pointed toward the door; flowers, ribbons, and candles in evidence. Women sang hymns and the men burned incense and candles.

Funerals were somber affairs, with the burial always outside the city. A popular new idea came into being, with the making of a death mask by covering the face of the deceased with molten wax and then removing it after it cooled, thus retaining a record of the features of the departed by the use of plaster paris or another material to form a more permanent image, such as bronze or lead.

Cremation was the most common method of disposal. Around the third century, A.D., underground burial became more popular. Funerals and burials in Rome were marks of the accomplishment of the deceased, and if you had a famous parent or sibling, you wanted everyone to know. Graves with impressive monuments were placed along roads entering the city where the deceased had lived. Remember, the reasons for the show were not religious but in recognition of the importance or stature reached in life. The cost of the burials and monuments used were astronomical and recognized as status symbols by everyone. At a time when a Roman soldier made 1000 sestries in a year, 500,000 or 1,000,000 sestries were spent by others on burials and related expenses. As one involved with funerals and burials for over forty years, I find it impossible not to remark that many of the practices and desires of families of the dead still find these same things important and well-worth spending an amount many would call a small fortune to provide the casket, vault, burial space, monument and funeral service of a loved one. The cost of a funeral and burial remains high and growing, just as the cost of our cars, vacations, home, boats, and second homes. As old men have said throughout history, I say where will it end? At the same time, I expect old men to feel that way a thousand years from now. How many of us can compare what seemed a fortune in Roman times to the $8,000 to $20,000 and up that some families are paying today for a funeral and burial.

Some historic authorities consider the beginning and others consider the end of the Roman Empire as the beginning of the Middle Ages or Medieval times. If we refer to a timeline of man, we find that modern form of Homo Sapiens first appear about 195,000 years ago, with man continuing to evolve through the Cro-Magnon stage where the use of bone and antler and other implements for making clothing, engraving and sculpture were in use. At about 30,000 years ago, paleontologists consider modern man to be found in certain areas of the globe including northern Africa, The Mid East, The Far East and parts of Europe and northern Asia.

We are accepting the timeline that concludes that the Middle Ages were from about 350 A.D. until about 1450 A.D. The most significant contribution of this era to funeral practices is that greater numbers of people are living in smaller spaces, thus man had to contend with the dead in more massive numbers. Some of the obvious causes were war with armies reaching over hundreds of thousands on each side causing tens of thousands of wounded who had little possibility of survival as well as tens of thousands of killed. Improved ways of killing went from cross bows, the use of animals such as elephants, long bows, Greek fire (the napalm of the Middle Ages) castle sieges and catapults, the use of poisons, burning crop lands, armored knights and finally the invention of gunpowder first for portable cannons progressing to hand-held weapons and large guns over a period of a few hundred years. In addition to war and its atrocious losses, mass deaths came from famine and pestilence. One pandemic plague episode during the Middle Ages was thought to have caused 20,000,000 deaths in Europe only. Disease was far ahead of medical knowledge or practice. Plagues in these early times left us with the horror of the death carts, and the picking up of the dead from institutions and homes every morning. Stories of the efforts of doctors and other medical personnel, including those manning the death carts are inspiring. Even handling the clothing of the deceased let alone tending to their suffering was risking an equally horrible death, yet there were those who spent weeks and months caring for the victims. Caring was all that could be done, since no cures were available. Mass graves or huge funeral pyres were the destiny of almost all who were infected.

In military actions rudimentary care was not completely overlooked. As usual rank had its privileges even in death. Regular troops were normally buried in large mass graves that could cover great areas. Officers of high rank, commanders and rulers lost in battle were many times honored by individual graves, being carried on their shields or on two long poles attached by two cross pieces to the site. Even in these early times comment about the deceased was sometimes made and some form of marker listing the name of the remains perhaps with his rank or title. Burials at sea were of course common in naval battle. The bodies of sailors were usually enclosed in a weighted canvas, placed on a board under the flag they had served, and after an honor was shown by the firing of cannons or a musical salute, the remains slid from under the flag into the sea. Of course many naval personnel were also blown to bits or went down with their ships, making burial at sea less glorious, but just as effective.

This was the early beginning of the recognition that soldiers in battle longed for their loved ones to know their fate. One of the many efforts to meet this need came in the American Civil War, although it was in evidence much earlier. Soldiers either wrote or had someone else write for them their name and home address on a small slip of paper, which was attached to the back of their jacket or shirt by a safety pin. By World War I, soldiers were supplied with dog tags and armies were equipped with graves registration personnel in an effort to identify the dead and place them in graves in military cemeteries near great battlefields. I once visited such a cemetery near Verdun, France, the site of one of the bloodiest engagements of World War I. There was an immense cemetery with the graves of identified dead in row upon row of graves marked by military crosses. In addition there was a great building, called an ossuary, containing the unidentified bones of 15,000 men, buried in the columns of the building.

By World War II, graves registration was a separate organization with thousands of members, and their actions were effective in identifying the dead and shipping them home if requested by their families. They were in many places embalmed, dressed in uniforms and placed in sealed metal caskets and shipped from areas in all theatres of the war. I also had an opportunity to visit a beautiful cemetery, which had a memorial of marble pillars and a circular wall, which listed the names of unidentified men buried below the memorial. The graves of those identified spread over a vast area with each soldier having a cross showing their name, rank, serial number and home state. A cross for each of the dead had a Protestant, Catholic, or Jewish emblem above it. I have heard of many families who went to Europe or one of the Pacific cemeteries to make arrangements to have the remains of their loved one shipped home, but decided to leave them undisturbed when they saw the beauty and the quality of care the cemeteries received. All service men are eligible to be buried in a National Cemetery, and their spouse can be interred below them if they die prior to the death of the serviceman. If you ever have an opportunity to visit Arlington Cemetery or the Punch Bowl in Hawaii or one of the other major military cemeteries throughout the world, do not fail to do so. You will never forget such a visit. Just as impressive is The Naval Memorial above the USS Arizona in Pearl Harbor, Hawaii. Honors for American Servicemen at least since WWI and WWII require the remains being shipped home for burial be accompanied by another serviceman of equal or higher rank to the final resting place.

While this duty is better than being shot at, it is never the less tough duty. They are involved with families who were against the war that claimed their son or grandson; they demand the escort be in constant attendance, or that he leave at once. I am mentioning the minority; most of the families appreciated the escort's assistance and realize it was valuable to them. I remember once or twice when a friend of mine was hostess at the Holiday Inn in Terre Haute that I convinced the escort to stay at that hotel and to contact the hostess in the lounge and tell her I had sent them. They always returned saying they had enjoyed the best night of their lives, much less the best escort tour they had served!

A partial list of causes of mass death in the Middle Ages and throughout history would include small pox, cholera, flu (20,000,000 in post WW I), malaria, and yellow fever and even whooping cough and scarlet fever in their time. To this we must add glaciers, earthquakes, tornadoes, hurricanes, tidal waves, fires and famines. Within the last year from which I am writing, a tsunami and several major hurricanes and cyclones have made their power known with horrifying results.

The times in which we live provide us with highly developed medical protection, weather prediction, excellent treatment from injury, equipment to remove fallen buildings and debris, equipment with which to fight forest fires, mud slides, floods and avalanches. We seem to be prepared for anything, but we regularly find that we are not How could we have anticipated or been prepared for 9/11. Even today our resources are strained to handle massive natural death tolls every year, particularly in more remote parts of the world, but even in our own country as well events can occur that strain our massive resources.

I have strayed very far from the chronological coverage of our subject, and I am going to turn to some noted authorities to return to some excellent coverage of the care of the dead in the period of the Middle Ages.

People living in Medieval times had no means or medical resources or physical equipment to resist disease and disaster, but concern for the dead did exist although those who died in such enormous numbers rendered any such concern mostly worthless.

Let's take a look at funeral practices for normal and individual death. According to historians Joseph and Frances Gies, in their book, *Life in a Medieval City*, "When a burgher (resident of a town or burg) dies, a public crier is hired to announce his death and the time and place of burial. The doors of the house and of the death chamber are draped with black serge. Two monks from the abbey wash the body with perfumed water, anoint it with balsam and ointment, and encase it in a linen shroud, and then they sew it in a deerskin and deposit it in a wooden coffin. Draped in a black pall, the coffin is placed on a bier consisting of two poles with wooden crosspieces and taken to the church, attended by a cortege of clergy and black-clad mourners, the widow and family making loud and visible lament. The bier halts outside the chancel gates (if the dead man is a priest, the body is laid out within the chancel), and the Mourning Office is said the "Dirge," from *Dirige*, the first word of the first antiphon. When the mass is over, the priest removes his chasuble, censes the body and sprinkles it with holy water, says the Lord's Prayer, in which all join; and then he pronounces the Absolutions, a series of prayers and antiphons of forgiveness and deliverance from judgment.

"As the cortege proceeds to the church burial grounds, monks from the abbey lead the way with crosses, sacred books and thuribles, and mourners follow with candles. The latter are numerous, for the poor can earn alms by carrying candles in a rich man's funeral procession. When the place of burial is reached, the priest makes the sign of the cross over the grave, sprinkles it with holy water, and digs a shallow trench in the shape of the cross. The real grave digging is then done to the accompaniment of psalms. The wooden coffin is lowered, the final collect for forgiveness said, the grave filled in, and a flat tombstone installed. (Those who cannot afford coffins rent one, and the remains are buried without the coffin, another custom which still exists.)

"The procession returns to the church, singing the seven Penitential Psalms. For a time the tomb will be lighted with candles and a funeral lamp. In few years the bones may be lifted out of the grave and stacked, so that the spaces can be used again." (*Life in a Medieval City, pp. 74-75.*)

Some differences exist between Christian and Jewish customs as shown by David Rausch, in his book concerning Jews and Judaism (*Building Bridges*), describing Jewish burial custom:

"Since the body is a holy vessel, created in the image of God, it is treated with utmost respect. It is not left alone from the time of death to the funeral, and psalms are often recited in the same room. Jewish communities usually have Cheurah Kaddishas (Sacred Burial Societies), composed of groups of volunteers who wash and dress the body of the deceased and make arrangements for the burial. The act of pre-burial purification is called taharah. A few members wash the body lovingly and carefully with warm water from head to foot. Cheurah comes from the root word 'friend,' and this act is one of the greatest mitzvot one can perform. Blessings are even recited before washing to connote respect and to express sorrow for any unintended disrespectful washing, and so forth.

"Regardless of status, the deceased is dressed in a tachrichim, simple white shrouds made of cotton or linen. If a brutal disfiguring accident has occurred, where blood has soaked into the clothing, the deceased is not washed but is buried in the same clothes. This is because the blood is viewed as sacred and deserving of burial as well. Only burial in a wooden casket under the earth is permitted. Burial usually occurs within twenty-four hours, unless an extension is needed to bring in family members from out of town. A funeral may not be conducted on the Sabbath.

"The funeral is simple and dignified. There is no open casket and no makeup. At a Jewish funeral you will not hear anyone saying, "My, doesn't he look good?" or "How lovely she appears today!" The deceased is not "asleep" in the casket. The mourner is to come to grips with this fact, and between death and burial should be confronting the reality that death has occurred. He has denied himself (according to Tamudic law) eating meat, drinking wine or liquor, bathing for pleasure, shaving, haircuts, marital relations, self-adornment, parties, and festive meals. Even the study of the Torah with its accompanying joy has been prohibited. Now he faces the casket, surrounded by friends. Family and friends follow the casket to the cemetery. Some dirt is thrown by the mourner onto the casket when it is lowered into the ground. After the burial, friends prepare the mourners' first meal."

A Christian should realize that his new body, though possessing some identity with the one we now possess, will be a new "spiritual body" (1 Corinthians 15:35-44). Therefore, there is no need to take extreme measures to ensure that our earthly "shell" is preserved from change and decay. God will not need to gather up the scattered molecules of our original earthly bodies. 1 Thessalonians 4:13-18 does not imply that ashes in funerary urns or decayed or embalmed bodies in earthly graves will suddenly be reconstituted. Rather, the Resurrection is the wonderful occasion in which believers who have died will again be granted full bodily form, this time in a glorified, immortal body that can never again die or undergo decay.

The next era of time was known as the Renaissance, and it was noted for great art, the reign of several great leaders and, the appearance of several great religious, military, governmental and philosophical advances. Cities and countries increased in population and power. This led to even greater wars and conquests with attendant casualties and deaths. An effort was now being made to provide identification and burial in cases where it was possible, but even more massive battles and broader epidemics prevented such efforts in many cases.

As we have regularly pointed out, funeral and burial customs in the case of the leaders in all of these fields continued to find more ways to sanctify, memorialize, or worship such personages. High officers of the church were laid out (a term we have not yet used which meant dressed and prepared) with all of their jewels of office and power. They might lie in state for several days in a cathedral with thousands of their subordinates and parishioners filing by their bier in humble respect. Honors at least as high went to kings, emperors, and dictators of that day. Admirals and Generals who had led great naval and military campaigns had all of this as well as recognition by the firing of hundreds of cannons for up to twenty-one times. And we talk about expensive funerals! The Renaissance knew how to pay homage to its great personages. With people like Charlemagne, Voltaire, Bonaparte, Peter the Great, the English Kings, and the Great Khans there was a tremendous amount of such honor to spread around.

Another honor begun in this time was the burial of the great in the catacombs beneath the tremendous cathedrals of the time. Even greater recognition brought burial below the floor of such cathedrals or in crypts provided in the walls. Memorials to such near immortals were more than lavish. Their accomplishments were engraved on these memorials along with poems or script about them and their forrbears.

Speaking of unusual honors and recognition, one day we had arranged to have three funeral services in the same afternoon. This was rare and difficult for a firm our size with the equipment we had available. We were planning to use our older hearse/ambulance combination vehicle for the second and third funerals. The cemetery for the second funeral was a rural one and had only a single lane dirt road for both an entrance and exit. In an effort to keep the hearse from being blocked from the exit, I asked the vault company owner who was on the job to start the hearse and move it to where it would be the first vehicle to leave. In those days, starter buttons on all cars were on the floorboard, and on combination hearse/ ambulances so was the siren button. You guessed it. The vault man turned on the key and put his foot on the siren. Talk about an exiting committal service! That probably took the prize.

As for the masses and more normal humans, funerals increased in importance with church funerals, honors and burial in increasingly elaborate cemeteries with flowers, trees and statues in use. Underground burial was most common, but mausoleums were making their appearance. Processions tended to be more like parades, with family members and dignitaries present given places of honor. As in the manner of the Romans, life's accomplishments were recognized in the best funeral and burial a family could provide. Debt and bankruptcy attended many such occasions at every economic level.

Chapter 4

The Beginning of the Funeral Industry

While a great deal of time of a calendar nature passes prior to our next subject of discussion, there is not so much changing in funerals and burials. More and more people of lower economic means are able to provide acceptable funeral and burial arrangements. Civic entities and churches of many faiths are providing cemeteries and assisting families with proper arrangements. Funerals and burials are more and more an expected tribute to most people in more and more parts of the world. A wide gap still exists between the wealthy and famous and the poor and unknown, but it is very, very, slowly narrowing. Customs and cultural mores improve at a pace that is frustrating and they are even less rapid in funeral practices. My father, whom I considered an authority on most aspects of the business always believed that changes in the industry took much longer time to take effect than in other fields. As I mentioned above, the public expected and counted on funerals to be as they had previously known them. Changes which over fifty years could be dramatic were much slower over a decade or two. I can remember several customs that changed during my career. One custom to disappear was that of flower girls. Girls who were old enough carried flower baskets and formed a double line through which the pall bears carried the casket and the mourners led by the next of kin followed to the tent that was provided for everyone during the committal service. In many larger communities the use of a tent is much less universal. A memorial chapel is provided by the cemetery for the committal service with the casket being moved to the actual burial space after the service. Honorary pall bears are named less than they used to be. Vocal music at one time was used on almost all services, but it is reserved today mostly for the funeral of dignitaries. Recorded music is now widespread and has returned the human voice through sound equipment. In some cities there is no police protection for processions which has led to the lack of a funeral cortege to the cemetery. Those attending the funeral are either released at the place of service or asked to reassemble at the cemetery. While service or fraternal groups still offer participation in funerals, there use is in decline. All of these changes for better or worse have taken long periods of time to become accepted. Some have reflected safety considerations, a tendency toward simpler funerals, or different points of emphasis by families. It is my belief that most of these changes are just in line with our changing lives.

We are moving several hundred years ahead to consider what many familiar with the field consider the beginning of the funeral industry, because of a technical advance made common by a man filling a need long-desired. Just as all families of soldiers killed in all of the wars up to its time, the parents and other relatives of the dead in the American Civil War wished to be able to know the circumstances surrounding the death of their loved ones. The bodies of some of the young men had been being shipped home in boxes partially filled with ice and straw, so that they could be buried in their family or church burial grounds. The distance involved allowed this to be attempted, and there were some on either side who did it on their own. This continued even after the end of hostilities. Many on each side felt that the other was a foreign country, and one side was fighting toward that end. As an example of the feelings involved, there are no confederate dead in the National Cemetery at Gettysburg. Disinterring their own dead and transporting them home were highly unpleasant tasks and the efforts of those who used the ice-filled boxes described above did not improve the transfer much.

In the tradition of American ingenuity, in stepped an entrepreneur of the truest sense. His name was Dr. Thomas Holmes. He was a resident of New York City and had received his medical training at College of Physicians and Surgeons at Columbia University. During the course of his study, he worked in pharmacy and developed an effective embalming fluid which, when injected into cadavers made them more pleasant to work on and retarded putrefaction. At the beginning of the Civil War, Dr. Holmes saw that the use of embalming was the answer to shipping the remains of soldiers killed home to their families. He went directly to Washington, D.C., where he distributed thousands of leaflets to soldiers describing the benefits of his work. His public relations work might have been a little direct, but his idea was well received among the men and particularly their families.

His method of injecting the fluid directly into the body of the deceased soldier through the use of a rubber squeeze ball was very primitive and would have required several hours for each body, but the results were far better than the straw and ice method. Dr. Holmes traveled from one battlefield to another, keeping a record of the name, rank, and home of each of the men for whom he provided embalming service.

His reputation and fame grew a great deal when he embalmed the remains of Col. Elmer E. Ellsworth, who had been a clerk in President Lincoln's law office in Springfield, Illinois, and was killed as a security guard for the president while on duty. His remains were viewed by a Mr. W. A. Kelly and First Lady Mary Todd Lincoln in the East Room of the White House. Incidentally, Dr. Homes continued the discriminatory practices started, as we noted, by the Egyptians. He charged seven dollars for the embalming of an enlisted man and thirteen dollars for an officer. I have no idea how the embalming could have been that much different.

Dr. Holmes' services allowed the bodies to be placed in a box or coffin and shipped longer distances to their former homes. This service was very well received and many of the remains of soldiers, particularly from the North were shipped home in this manner either in wagons or by railroad. The preservation of the body allowed it to be viewed at home prior to burial in many cases. The parents, wives and other relatives of those young men felt that the burial in their church cemetery or their family plot relieved some of the hurt of their great loss. It is a process that today we call closure. Qualified and trained people are brought to the place of a disaster and attempt to assist survivors in accepting the loss of loved ones. I was never exposed to this practice, although we constantly attempted to provide this service as laymen. Suppose a young couple lost a set of twins in their third year. No one could doubt that this couple needed some help, but in small towns in Indiana there was usually no one more that a minister, priest or physician. Of course, everyone including the funeral director did or said what they could but experience probably did not replace special training plus experience. Speaking of experience, it seemed to me and to almost all of those I associated with in funeral work that the loss of a child or children was the most difficult thing for survivors to handle. There is no such thing as an easy death, we are never ready to lose our parents or a sibling, but the loss of a child seems the most difficult to accept.

And so, we are nearing the completion of our journey of 30,000 years. There is still a long, long way to go in the development of the funeral industry, but Dr. Holmes and others who followed him made great strides. The beginning of arterial embalming, as the procedure was and still is called brought about four worth while reasons for its use: Sanitation, Preservation, Restoration, and Presentation. Sanitation meant that the human body could be prevented from infecting the living with the disease from which they had died in almost all cases. The body could be retained for several days or weeks for funeral arrangements or transportation to other parts of the country through preservation. Restoration was intended to bring a more normal appearance to a body which had been disfigured or damaged by the cause of death. Such work would have been required in most of Dr. Holmes' cases. Presentation implies the deceased is in a condition, through positioning, cosmetics, care of the hair and proper clothing to be viewed by family and friends during the visitation and funeral.

Embalming has always remained something of a mystery to many people, even today. I'm going to explain it in a rudimentary fashion. The embalmer, who must be licensed in all states after proper training, makes an incision through the skin at one of six normal places named after the arteries that lie in these locations fairly close to the surface. The locations are called the left and right carotid spaces, the left and right axillary spaces, and the left and right femoral spaces. In each of these spaces lies the artery of that name along with a vein and a nerve called by the same term. The embalmer raises the artery and vein from the space he chooses to use and cuts open a space in each. A metal arterial tube is inserted into the artery and embalming fluid is injected under pressure toward the heart, thus forcing the blood from the veins which had been opened and then from the body thru a drainage tube of a flexible material, usually rubber, into a channel along the side of the table and into the sewer.

Embalming fluid which is composed of from eight to fourteen percent formaldehyde along with several other ingredients including alcohol, formalin, and phenol, circulate throughout the body under pressure where the formaldehyde converts to its natural state as a gas, escapes from the arteries mainly through the capillaries and kills most of the bacteria in the tissues which cause decomposition.

Accidental deaths and autopsies bring about variations to this process. In accidents, if limbs or portions of the body are damaged or lost, injections might have to be made in several of the arterial spaces. In autopsies, which can be in the abdominal, thoracic (chest) or cranial areas, the internal organs are removed as they were by the Egyptians! Fluids are removed to dry the cavities that are then covered by a drying and preserving agent. The viscera are immersed in an embalming fluid with a much higher content of formaldehyde (as much as 50%), and the viscera (internal organs) are replaced and the incisions of the doctor performing the autopsy are closed and sealed. If neither an accident nor autopsy is involved, vacuum pressure is used through a hollow tube to remove as much fluid as possible from the body cavities and the stronger fluid is injected into the body by the same tube.

In addition to the techniques described above, the head and the limbs are placed in the desired position. The eyes are closed by using perforated caps and a metal device called an injection needle is used to close the mouth. Some embalmers prefer to close both the eyes and mouth by suturing with surgical thread. Of course this work is all done after the remains are bathed and cleaned. The work is done on an embalming table, which provides drainage into a sink which directs the fluids into the sewer system of the building in which the work is performed. This roughly completes the embalming procedure.

After the embalming has been completed in most cases cosmetics are used, as well as a hairdresser for ladies and a barber for men in an effort to provide lifelike appearances to the deceased, which most families seem to desire. Another interesting thing that is not well known is that if embalming is completed before rigor mortis takes effect the extremities of the body will assume a rigidity, which is a stiffening of the joints of the arms, legs, and neck. If rigor mortis is in effect prior to embalming, then this stiffening does not occur and the limbs remain flexible.

Rigor mortis is a natural condition, which occurs from four to twelve hours after death, depending on the conditions of the body, the temperature at the location of the death, and a few other factors such as the weight of the corpse. Rigor mortis is a condition recognized by friends and family of the deceased and gives an indication that death has occurred. Another sign is called post mortem lividity, and refers to a darkening of the lower areas of the body, and is simply a staining of the skin due to the blood within the body seeking the lowest part of the body due to gravity. Another sign of death is the cooling of the remains.

Since there is a relaxation of all of the muscles of the body at death, the jaws, limbs and neck all assume a flaccid condition, which, as mentioned above is changed by the embalming procedure if it occurs prior to rigor mortis. While state laws vary in regard to embalming, most are similar to that of Indiana, where embalming is only required if a deceased person dies of a communicable disease and is to be shipped over a state line. While we are on the subject of legal requirements, every state requires a death certificate, which is usually signed by the attending physician and indicates his opinion of the cause of death. In cases where there is no attending doctor or where he is not sure of the cause of death, the county Health Officer becomes responsible to determine it following an investigation. If there is evidence of foul play or an accident involved then the coroner of the county becomes responsible for the investigation and signing the certificate in either case, an autopsy is many times used to confirm the determinations. In larger cities the health department may have a large staff of investigators, medical personnel and legal representatives. Most of the remaining information on the death certificate is personal information regarding the deceased, such as name, address, occupation, parents' names and, of course the place of burial. Even in cases of cremation, the final disposition of the remains must be shown. In cases where cremation is used, there is a delay before disposition can occur. When the certificate is acceptable to the Board of Health, a Burial Permit shows the place of burial. If the burial involves removal from the state in which the death occurred, then a new burial permit must be issued from the receiving state through the county in which the burial takes place. All of the information from the death certificate is used for statistical purposes such as number of deaths from certain diseases or percentages of deaths that are accidents, suicides, murders, or of natural causes.

Honor services for military personnel or former military personnel are the same for all ranks and branches of the service. Military Post Guards of Honor, and Military Cemeteries such as the Punch Bowl in Hawaii and Arlington Cemetery just outside Washington D.C. provide grandeur and precision second to none, but many American Legion Posts and other military organizations perform the Burial Ceremony including the flag presentation and sounding of taps. The ceremony is impressive and every honorably discharged or active serviceman is entitled to the service. Whether it is provided by the crack, chrome plated, white webbed, fully uniformed honor squad from a military post or by a local VFW or American Legion Post in some small town, the ceremony provides memories for the family of the deceased serviceman or veteran. The ceremony places a solemn feeling on the proceedings of the burial of a military man. I can remember several occasions where the local Legion provided these services in atrocious weather conditions, heat, snow, rain, or wind the honor squads carried on. Once at Center Ridge Cemetery in Sullivan Indiana, I remember we were interring the remains of a veteran in the small mausoleum located there. The temperature was about zero inside the mausoleum where the minister was conducting the committal service but it was about fifteen below and windy where the Legion Squad was formed for the firing squad and taps. It seemed to be the longest service I had ever heard; I could only imagine how those outside were suffering.

A certified copy of the Death Certificate from the Board of Health is accepted as to the proof of death and it is used for legal matters such as transfer of property or in criminal trials. All counties are to require burial permits issued prior to the deceased being removed from the county. While all of the information above seems a little complex, most deaths are routine, with the funeral director securing a signed death certificate from the doctor, presenting it at the Board of Health and receiving a burial permit, which is given to the official of the cemetery.

I want to comment a bit on the relationship between funeral practices in small communities such as my family operated and those found in larger cities which of course may vary from a few thousand to several million. There is a great variation in each group in such things as number of funerals handled in a year, number of employees at a location, number of businesses under one ownership, and means of handling pre-need funerals, limited service funerals, cremations, and transfers to other locations.

I have the records of McHugh Funeral Home(s) from its beginning in 1908 up to the present time, when my family no longer has anything to do with the business, although our name still appears on a sign in front of two of the locations. I discovered a few years ago that as a part of the sale of the business, I had been compensated for the use of our family name by the business that purchased it forever. I wish this had not been a part of the sale, but I agreed to it at the time.

Information in the early records of the business indicate the first funeral provided by the McHugh Funeral Home was in January 1908. The total charge, which was broken down as a charge for a casket, $68.00, Embalming, $5.00, Slippers and hose, $2.50 and $2.00 was paid to the minister, for a total of $85.50. The payment to the minister was later called cash advanced and might include musicians, flowers, cemetery lot, grave opening and other charges such as unusual transportation when required. An interesting aspect of the cash advance system was, if you were never paid for a funeral, you not only lost the cost of the merchandise provided, the value of your time, but also the cash outlay you had made on behalf of the family.

The second funeral listed was overpaid by $23.00. At this time the families paid virtually all the funerals in cash. It might be in one or three or fifteen payments but they were cash from the family. There is no indication of life insurance proceeds, union, company or federal or state death benefits. Neither is their any evidence of poor relief programs. Not too many years later all the above became a regular form of payment or partial payment. In 1924, I see a payment made by the union local in the amount of $75.00. Lodge and company benefits and "Soldier" payments begin to appear. Very soon embalming is up to $6.00 and a charge of $10.00 begins to appear for the use of the hearse. I never knew when our firm began to supply ambulance services but a charge for $3.00 for ambulance service can be found prior to 1920. A charge for burial vaults shows up very early and charges for candles for use in Catholic funerals are found.

Most of the funerals from the beginning until the end of the 1920s run from less than $100.00 to a little over $200.00, with great emphasis on the lower figure. We should also mention stillborn, infant and child funerals. The records show only a charge of $8.00 to $25.00 for a casket. I can remember my father, whose entry into the business we will discuss a little later, telling me that caskets from 1 foot six inches up to adult size were stocked in increments of one foot. There were many, many childhood deaths and it took some little time to get a baby casket made in a special size. By the time I entered the business, we only carried caskets for stillborn babies, since improved medical service had nearly eliminated all other deaths of infants except accidents and a special size casket could be secured in a matter of hours. While no funerals were ever marked by pleasure, the funeral of a child was very often heart wrenching and crying and other evidence of sadness and shock was much in evidence.

We'll check the records of the funeral home as the years go by to note any new services or products, but before we finally get to our main story of the operation of three funeral homes in three small towns in Indiana, we have to discuss the wide range of businesses and how they varied in operation.

Chapter 5

The Industry Grows

After the Civil War and due to the acceptance of embalming by the public the funeral business began to grow in the United States. As with most service and commercial businesses, the lead was taken by the firms in the larger cities. A larger market and probably an easier acceptance to new ideas led to this more rapid growth. Firms started and most were successful. A few began in the 1860s and by the '80s most cities had many competing businesses. As in all such situations, some grew into large and wealthy organizations and many failed to make the grade. Although the cities might be huge, the funeral businesses tended to appeal to religious, ethnic, labor, or fraternal neighborhoods. The firms that were able to appeal to several or all such groups grew into the giants. There were many such firms that expanded horizontally into related services such as cemeteries, vault manufacturers, casket construction, and flower shops.

There was a lot of politics involved as in all such service related businesses, and for a long time, almost all funeral firms were also into ambulance (a great many still are) service, which lent itself even more to political connection. Contacts could be made with police departments, hospitals, medical groups, and fraternal, civic, political, religious, and social organizations. Such successful connections led to enormous funeral and funeral related companies.

As a general rule, not until the 1870s or 1880s or so did funeral homes begin to be established in small towns. The businesses in these communities had to appeal to all such groups of people. However, in many towns that had mostly Catholic and Protestant churches, there would be two firms in each town attempting to serve one or the other religion. Small town firms could be very small in the number of services conducted. Some existed, and some still do based on thirty or forty funerals a year. Many of these firms were operated by part time funeral directors who might have another related or unrelated business or occupation. Almost any combination could exist. I was in the auto parts business for quite a long time, while operating our three funeral homes. I thought it was funny to say, "If some one figured out a way to keep from dying they will probably have trouble with their car." In addition to operating a separate business, many small town operators would try to locate in nearby communities that had no funeral home or seemed to be large enough to support another. I can remember while traveling with my wife and children driving through a small to medium sized town, I would try to guess the number of funeral homes in the town. We would then get our motel room and everyone would run to the telephone book to see how close I had come to the actual number. The size of a community in which any firm operated was, of course, very pertinent to their growth.

To open a new place was a difficult thing, bringing such considerations as the possible growth of the community, the proper location for the building, nearness to the hospital and cemeteries, the size and cost of the structure you were planning, and the number of employees and vehicles you would need. Then again, a decision in regard to ambulance service would have to be made. While many firms, in all sizes of communities, were very successful in operating ambulance service, many other firms provided the service because it was expected of a funeral home.

Many years after the time we are now considering, special requirements and operating restrictions for ambulance service forced the funeral business to decide whether to remain or get out of the ambulance service. Some still operate very successful ambulance operations, but many, many others gave up the service. Let me tell you why we got out. We were located in from one to three towns, with the owner or one employee in each location. Ambulance service was 24 hours a day, 7 days a week, and a major US Highway ran through two of the three towns and a State Highway right thru the other. We were using what was called "Combination" hearses and ambulances. The attendant seats in the ambulance folded into the floor and there was a set of locking hooks to hold the cot. You removed the cot and the attaching hooks and folded the seats into the floor and your ambulance became a hearse. There were even removable hearse curtains that could be added for appearance and a platform with rollers allowed the casket to be placed in the hearse. We had no training in the ambulance field. Our instructions from our local doctors were to "pick'em up and get'em to the hospital," where they might remain on your cot for an hour or more while waiting for a doctor or receiving emergency care treatment. No consideration was given to your time, even if you had funerals going.

But the two major reasons for getting out of the business was the 24/7 and the extremely poor pay at that time. In our small county of less than twenty thousand people, I now sometimes notice a transfer of funds to the Ambulance Service of $75,000 or a $100,000 in addition to the annual budget. The last year I was in the ambulance service, my gross income was $3,300. We were paid a pittance for patients on welfare and in case of an emergency nature; you had to drop everything, whenever you were called. You actually operated the 24/7 ambulance service and provided the vehicles as a part of your business. When I see a bill for an ambulance for a few blocks, which might be for five hundred dollars or more, I cringe. Of course, the personnel and equipment they provide today make the service more like an emergency room on wheels and they probably save more lives by their training and equipment than we lost by our lack of training and equipment.

Let me tell you a few stories about our ambulance experiences. I will never forget them. The first ambulance call I ever made was at the age of fifteen (no driver's license). No one could locate my father, and someone had seen me going into the local theatre. They came after me and I got the ambulance and took a young girl of about my age that had been kicked in the head by a horse to the hospital in our county seat. That was about sixty years ago, and the girl I transported is still alive and a good friend of mine. My second ambulance call was when one of my best friend's mother, who lived next door to the funeral home shot herself in the throat. The young boy (he was four years younger than I) and I took his mother to the same hospital, where she was pronounced dead, probably from choking to death on her own blood. I'm pretty sure my lack of training and experience might have contributed to her death, but you did the best you could (I was still fifteen).

Many of the experiences I remember the most relate to accidents on the highway. Once I pulled up to a single car accident, and a lady was wedged up under the dashboard of the car. I got the cot all arranged next to the door of the car (this is not as easy as it sounds, you had to figure which side you were going to lift from, and not get the cot between you and the person you were moving.) When I got everything set, two or three people in the crowd that was always present said, "Hey you can't move her, you might injure her further!" I got the cot and started to place it back in the ambulance. The same people said, "what in the world are you doing?" and I said, "You told me not to touch her; I'm going back to bed." They, of course, realized someone had to move her, and they were stuck with me. Once, less than five hundred yards from where the above incident occurred, I was called to pick up two young ladies who had died in an accident when they had left the road and hit a telephone pole. After I got one of the bodies of the girls on the cot and placed the other in an auxiliary stretcher we usually carried, I saw a human hand lying among some covers on the floor of the car. I looked at the two bodies that I had moved and found they each had both their hands. There was another girl's body beneath the covers on the floorboard. I placed her body on the front seat and put her head in my lap and took off for the hospital, although I felt sure they were all three dead. When you got to the site of a wreck, it was always a pleasure to see that a state trooper or an officer from the county Sheriff's office was already there. These guys would take over, get traffic moving, help with crowd control, and assist you in loading the injured or dead. If I couldn't have a trooper of some sort at the scene, my next choice would be a truck driver. I found them to be of great assistance in any way they could help and a few of them were almost always there ahead of me. They carried torches for traffic warning and helped in the loading. Later on, they all had C-B radios and could contact police, hospitals, wreckers, or anyone else that might be needed.

Many funeral directors I knew were attracted to the business by a desire to drive an ambulance with a siren and a red light at 90 miles an hour. This never appealed to me. I did it because it was a tough part of my job. It was my experience, for the most part, that you had to wait at the hospital for assistance for a longer time than you could have possibly saved by driving that fast. You also ran a risk of injuring yourself, your passenger, your patient(s), or someone in another vehicle. About the only time I drove fast was when a child had been injured, and his or her parents were with you. They expected haste and I could understand that. I want to mention providing ambulance service for the coalmines in the area.

You will remember at one time there were seven mines near Shelburn. Through the years we shared with other funeral homes in providing the mines with ambulance service. I'm sure my grandfather and father were involved in hundreds of mine accident cases. By the time I was in charge we were down to three or four mines near Shelburn and Hymera, but one of them was a big one. That was Thunderhead Mine about two or three miles from Shelburn. Several hundred miners were employed there and accidents were rather frequent. The area was considered to have a "bad top," which meant a lot of roof cave-ins. The main thing I remember about coal miners was they were tough as hell. They seldom expressed evidence of their pain, although they had previously made a trip on a mine car for several miles before they could be brought up the slope of the mine in a wire basket suspended by ropes from an endless chain. All this was before I had them on my cot. I remember a particular miner (I even remember his name) whose leg was severed and hanging together only by skin (Someone had applied a tourniquet). He did not utter a sound as we moved him to the ambulance and hauled him to the hospital. I heard he was just as tough while learning to live with an artificial limb.

I can recall many mine accident calls. There was one thing that didn't work out at Thunderbird. If the victim was conscious, they were allowed to pick the hospital where they wanted to be admitted. While I didn't see anything wrong with the policy, I sometimes was gone four or five hours on trips I expected to be one hour, since there were miners driving many miles to work, and they wanted to go to the nearest hospital to their home. All in all, my memories of the ambulance service are of hard work, long hours, and a feeling of inadequacy. These feelings were sometimes partially relieved by a letter of thanks from a patient or his family. I remember on at least one occasion when the medical authorities set up a demonstration of the facilities to get injured men to the hospital. We were all warned this was going to happen, but we were not told when. All of the firms that provided ambulances were a little more on edge. All of the equipment was spotless, someone was always next to the ambulance. Since I handled the Thunderbird calls on a regular basis (work had leaked out the imitated tragedy was to the there) I certainly wanted to show up first. Medical people agreed to act out the accident scene at the shop of Thunderbird Mine. The big day arrived and I managed to reach the scene first. The "injured" were lying in all sorts of positions with bandages, slings and crutches and plenty of assumed blood everywhere. I selected two badly "injured men," placed them in the ambulance and was told to beat a path for the hospital. I would have done so if it had been real, but I wasn't going to risk my equipment, the "patients," other drivers or myself for any play acting. I got to the hospital in plenty of time for the system to be judged, but I hadn't put anyone at risk.

Two more stories about the ambulance and then we're moving on. My father and I went once to the home of a lady who was in labor to take her to the hospital for delivery. She did not want to go! She really did not want to go! My father and I managed to wrestle her onto the cot and used our belts to tie her down. As we were starting to leave the door of her bedroom she managed to get each foot braced against each side of the doorjamb. Well, we pulled and she pushed and lo and behold, the baby was born. My father took over, he laid the baby on the mother's lap and we proceeded directly to the hospital. Both mother and Baby did fine. My father handled it pretty well, but I nearly had apoplexy.

The County Judicial Department once called and asked us to pick up a bachelor whom we knew to be a rough guy with a violent temper who hit the bottle on most of his good days. We went to his home where several people were in attendance to see what happened. We placed the cot and my father told the man we were there to take him to the hospital. He said he wasn't going. My father replied he was going to go, since we had orders from the judge. The man repeated, "I'm not going." My father said, "Yes you are!" He then pulled the covers from the man and discovered about a 12-inch butcher knife in his hand. My father, who was something of a wag, said, "Well maybe you're not going!" We left instead and called the Judge and told him to send some better men than us. He sent the state police.

This was, of course, back in the days when doctors did many house calls. Sometimes the doctors, who received many more calls than we did, would receive a call where someone was reporting a member of the family appeared to have died. If the doctor knew the family well and trusted their judgment, he would sometimes tell them to call their funeral director, have them come and call back if the patient wasn't dead! Life was simpler then!

Once my father and I were called to the home of a friend of mine's Dad's residence, we arrived there, looked over the remains, secured the usual first call information, and placed the body in the hearse. When we got into the front seat, my father mentioned that he couldn't be absolutely sure that the gentlemen was dead and asked how I felt. When I replied that I felt the same way, he said he would get in the back and re-move the cover from the man's face and for me to drive to the hospital. We were fortunate that there was a doctor there, and a nurse described our situation. The doctor brought a stetho-scope to the car and pronounced the man dead. He then said that he had often thought if he wanted to murder someone he would do it in Sullivan County, since all the funeral directors snatched up every one who didn't move! After digesting this comment, my father and I wondered what the doctor would have had us do differently. Should we have called him or a competitor and asked them to drive fifteen or twenty miles in the middle of the night to pronounce someone dead? All in all, we felt we had handled things rather well. We never told the family about this, since we had made the right call. This gentleman's son was a close, personal friend of mine, who is now also deceased.

I have probably given the impression that I have changed the subject of the book to that of ambulance service but such is not the case. We are still coming to the story of the operation of one to three small funeral homes in southwestern Indiana.

From my grandfather beginning in 1908, he operated the location in Shelburn as sole proprietor. In the days during and immediately after the First World War he was able to support his family full time in the business. My father's sisters were married and one moved to Centralia, Illinois and the other just about six miles south of Shelburn. Each of their husbands worked in the food distribution industry. My father married a young lady who had taught school for one year in a rural school with eight grades of students in one room.

My mother was a small lady and many of the students were much larger than she was. This did not lead to easy discipline. One student, an eighth grade boy, once kicked her black and blue. When he became a man he apologized to her and became a friend. I think my mother was required to attend teaching college for six months to qualify for this teaching position. One thing was for sure; she was immediately on her own. She lived with a family near the school where she took her meals, and drove their horse and buggy to school Not only did she teach, but also she was responsible for cleaning the school and tending the fire in the stove in winter. I can remember my parents talking about courting under those conditions. They ended the living, courting and teaching conditions after one year by their marriage. I never suggested to either of them that the job might have encouraged the marriage. When you relate some of these stories they bring two things to mind. You are getting old and times have changed a great deal.

Chapter 6

Our Family Business Grows

My father had been graduated from high school in Sullivan in 1918. He always bragged that he spent two years in seventh grade. He was too young for service in World War I and was also later too old for service in World War II. He decided to attend Embalming School in Indianapolis and enter business with my grandfather. I think I have heard the period of time required was six weeks to complete the course. When I went in 1953, it was two years to learn embalming. A great deal happened to my family and the funeral business in the next few years. Shortly after my father graduated from embalming school he entered business with my grandfather. They soon were able to purchase an existing funeral business in the nearby town of Hymera, Indiana.

I'm going to digress again to explain the well-accepted origin of the name of the town of Hymera. The community had been first known as Little Pittsburg, due to the smoke and coal dust that came from surrounding coal mines. When the town was organized and had a Post Office, the first postmistress was a lady by the name of Mary. Of course all residents had to pick up their mail each day or when it was convenient, since there was no mail delivery there and still isn't. Everyone entering the office greeted the lady in charge with a hearty "Hi! Mary"; thus the name of the town became Hymera. You would have to search very hard to find a town or city of the same name.

The purchase of the business in Hymera occurred in about 1920 and my parents were ensconced in a residence next to a business building that served as a funeral home. By 1922, my sister was born and the business was called McHugh Funeral Homes, with my grandfather operating the Shelburn location and my father, still a very young man, in charge of the Hymera branch. Ambulance service was provided in both communities. By the middle '20s, total funeral cost ran from $350 or $375, if you subtracted the cash advance items, many were still under $300. A charge was still rare for opening the grave, so it must have been a service still provided by friends of the family for nothing. Where a charge does appear, it is for six dollars. Funerals were still almost all paid for by cash from the family, although the records sometime show payment by a local union of fifty or one hundred dollars. The state benefit or "soldier's claim," as it was called, was seventy-five dollars.

Each of the towns had a business building for a funeral home, with a room for embalming, a display room for a selection of caskets, and a small office where the families could meet with the funeral director to make funeral decisions as to time, place, and hour of service. Visitations (wakes) were still in the residence of the deceased for the most part, and the funeral was also there unless it was at the family church. By rearranging the furniture and changing the business building there was space of a sort to conduct a funeral if it was the wish of the family to use the business building.

Our area is more than amply supplied with cemeteries. Sullivan County, a county never in excess of much over 22,000 in population during my lifetime had over three hundred cemeteries. While many of these cemeteries were family or church owned, that is still an amazing number. Many were allowed to overgrow with weeds and get in a terrible condition. A number of years later a state law was passed requiring the trustees of each township to provide upkeep of all cemeteries that did not have funds of their own for that purpose.

Both Shelburn and Hymera had very old cemeteries by the time our family entered into business. Hymera had several cemeteries surrounding the town, Bethel Cemetery is across the state highway from the Bethel Methodist Church, and the Knights of Pythias Cemetery, commonly called K of P, is about a mile east of town. This cemetery was turned over to the town a number of years ago, the Case Cemetery, just east of K of P had been added to it and also placed under operation of the town. The community faces a problem as of this writing because Bethel Cemetery has been full for a long time, and space in the K of P is almost gone and most available space is in the Case Cemetery, which was never very large.

While I have not mentioned the third town in southwestern Indiana in which we operated a funeral home because we have not reached the date it was purchased in a chronological sense, I will mention that it was and is served by an excellent cemetery with a continuously active Board of Directors. The cemetery is called West Lawn, and it is located about a mile southwest of the third town, Farmersburg, Indiana. The cemetery has adequate space, an excellent site, is well kept, and

Flag Display recently added at West Lawn Cemetery, Farmersburg.

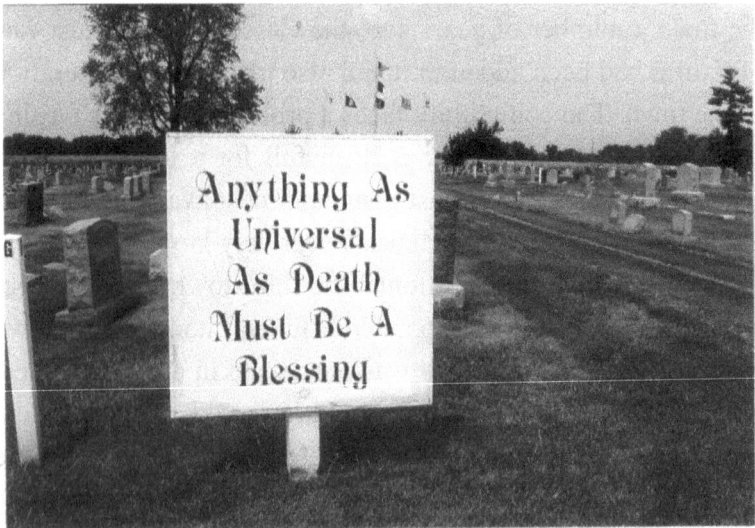

Anything As
Universal
As Death
Must Be A
Blessing

Sign at entry of West Lawn Cemetery,
which once gave the cemetery national publicity.

should supply the needs of the community into the foreseeable future. They have recently put up a nice display of governmental and military flag, and they are constructing a memorial chapel for committal services. I have advised a couple of the directors of the cemetery that while a chapel is a wonderful idea, they should be prepared for the families of the deceased to either drive by the actual burial space as they leave the cemetery or return shortly thereafter to the site. I have noticed this in most of the committal services I have had that were in a chapel. I believe that to the families closure can only come at the actual space where the remains of their loved one is placed.

There are several other changes mentioned above that families accept only because they have to. One is the absence of police protection from the place of the service to the entrance of the cemetery. This has been a gradual change over the years that has varied in different communities, but it has included families paying for protection from off-duty officers, organizations other than actual police providing protection, funeral processions trying to remain in contact with each other without any protection, or just giving up and meeting at the cemetery with no connection during the trip. Cost is, of course, at the basis of this problem, and funeral homes try using signs on the public vehicles and lights on the lead car and hearse, but it causes a great deal of trouble, since some drivers not in the procession recognize it as a funeral and want to show respect and a great many others do not.

Thinking about processions to and in cemeteries reminds me of another actual happening that occurred during a funeral for a stillborn child. It seemed to me that many of the stillborn babies were born to parents of limited means, so over the years I tried to keep costs of these funerals as low as possible. I had no tent, chairs, or lowering device for such funerals. I didn't use the hearse, usually placing the little casket on the lap of the grandparents in their own car, and taking any flowers in the trunk of that car or in whatever vehicle I was driving. I kept a small piece of imitation grass in the garage to cover the dirt pile and the open grave, just using a couple of small sticks to support the casket during the committal service. I explained to each family my reasons for these measures was to keep costs as low as possible for the parents. Almost everyone approved of this, except in the last years of my career when employers' medical plans sometimes carried death benefits on all members of the family regardless of age. On the occasion I am describing the family was receptive to my plan and we were using it to keep costs low.

We arrived at the cemetery, and I removed the few, small floral tributes from the trunk of my car, and proceeded to assist the grandparents in departing their car while carrying the small casket between them. I noticed I could not easily carry the 5 or 6 small flower baskets by myself, so I turned to a little girl of about four or five years of age and asked if she would like to help me carry the flowers to the grave, which was 50 or 75 feet away. The little girl was thrilled, asked for and received permission from her parents, and I handed her two baskets, feeling I could handle the others. I had already placed the grass over the grave and dirt pile. The little girl and I started with the flowers, the grandparents carrying the casket followed, with other relatives and friends bringing up the rear. I reached the site first and began placing the flowers around the covered dirt pile and grave. I then turned to assist the grandparents, only to discover to my bewilderment that my little flower bearer had fallen into the grave. As you can imagine, this stirred quite a commotion. I pulled the little girl from the grave, attempted to remove the mud from her frock, placed the casket in position, apologized to everyone, and requested the minister to complete the committal. I am seventy-seven years old as of this writing, and I have remembered this event for probably thirty-five years and if I live for another thirty-five years, I will NEVER forget it. I hope everyone else concerned has forgotten or forgiven it.

Another occasion comes to mind when I used equipment normally used for funeral in an unusual way. Several years ago some friends and I formed a poker club. In order to make the idea more palatable to our wives we withheld twenty-five cents (it was a small poker game) which was intended to provide a party for the members and their wives at the end of the season, which was to be in the spring. One member kept the draw in a cloth bag, which we discovered to our dismay only held about $200 when we called it quits for the year. A party for seven or eight couples on $200 might have to be held at the ice cream shop, so gamblers that we were, we used the money to buy a driver in the Indianapolis 500 mile race that Memorial Day. If I remember correctly, and I think I do, the driver was A. J. Foyt, who won several 500's during his career. We had picked him on one of his good years and our $200 had grown to about $1200 or $1400, which put the party on an entirely different level. The whole bunch drove about 75 miles to a town which had a Holiday Inn in the days of Holidome Inns, and there was an excellent German restaurant several blocks away. We gambled all afternoon on a small golf course in the Holidome and then decided it was time to head for the German restaurant.

Everyone had a shower and as we were loading up for the trip to the restaurant, I remembered I had the funeral flags for cars in the trunk of my car, so I got them out, placed them on top of every car we were using and we took off. The town is a great one and this was a long time ago, so everyone coming toward us pulled over to their side of the road, people on cross streets stopped so that we could go through red lights and we pulled up at the front of the restaurant where sympathetic valet parkers helped us unload and get into the restaurant while we struggled mightily to keep from laughing out loud.

I pulled this stunt once at a New Year's dance, placing the flags on the tables of groups who didn't seem to be having a super time. I put one on the table of a group who included another funeral director I barely knew, and he didn't think it was a bit funny, although everyone else in that area of the dining hall had a great laugh. I removed his sign, and that went over well also. Fun is where you find it, I guess.

I think it was in 1956 that my wife, our only son at that time and I traveled by train to a city in Mississippi, where we picked up a new Pontiac Hearse/Ambulance combination and drove it home. We were on the cutting edge of style since the car was painted in a pale shade of green and would be the sharpest vehicle around. I only had the car in the garage a night or two when I got a call that a gentleman had driven his vehicle into an embankment just south of Little Flock Cemetery.

I hurried down there and looked the situation over. The man was unconscious, with serious head and neck injuries. With some help from bystanders, I got the gentleman on the cot and into the new ambulance, where I hate to admit that I noticed that he was bleeding profusely on the floor of our new ambulance. I turned to the man who lived on the corner and asked if he had a towel that I could borrow. He brought me one immediately, and I hastened to wrap it around the neck of the injured man to spare the floor of the new pale green ambulance from the blood of the injured driver.

I hastened the car to the hospital, where they began the examination of the gentleman. Soon the doctor in charge asked, rather tersely, "Who put this towel around this man's neck?" After thinking a moment, I replied, "I guess I'll have to admit I put the towel on, Doc!" He was a rather brusque guy, and he said, "It's a damned good thing you put it on, McHugh, this guy's got a ruptured jugular vein. You just saved his life!"

This reminds me of our complete lack of training. We had a first-aid course in Mortuary School and that was it. Compared to today's ambulance personnel, we were as infants doing a job as best we could. Experience in this field only went so far.

The cemetery for Shelburn is in reality two separate cemeteries. One was located in Hamilton Township, just south of Shelburn, and the other was organized in 1821 and located next to the Little Flock Baptist Church, from which it takes its name. The cemeteries were adjacent to each other. Many years ago Little Flock took over the maintenance of the Hamilton Township section, and much more recently the grave of an American Revolutionary soldier was located in that section. After considerable correspondence with the Veterans Administration and with the assistance of the local American Legion Post, we were able to get a military monument to mark the grave of Albert Plough.

Sign and benches recently added in the center of Little Flock
Cemetery. There is a lighted American flag near this area.

Stone showing some of the history of
Little Flock Cemetery, which was established in 1821.
Indiana became a state in 1816.

Many years ago the Thompson family provided the original ground for Little Flock Cemetery. Over the years the Thompsons have made several additions to the cemetery. This family had been behind most of the progress of the cemetery, and a substantial donation from a daughter of the original organizers has solved the financial problems of the cemetery, at least for the present. A grandson and a great-grandson of this family are still on the cemetery board. The Thompsons have provided everything from administration to grave opening. The local funeral director handles the sale of lots, and locating graves at the time of need. This, of course, was my grandfather, father, and I from 1908 until 1984, but our successors have maintained the tradition. An old expression, "it goes with the territory," applies to the local funeral director when it comes to the operation of Little Flock Cemetery. To reaffirm this expression, I am still president of the Board, even though I sold the funeral business over twenty years ago. Little Flock is about eight and one-half acres in size, and in the next few years is going to be faced with finding additional space. I'm not sure where this is going to come from.

We have also improved Little Flock by adding a lighted flag and a new sign located near the center of the cemetery. We nave on order two stone benches which we are going to locate near a small granite monument on which we have engraved some of the history of Little Flock.

Among the records of Little Flock Cemetery, which are complex and composed of five sections on paper, there is a very interesting section called Accidental Deaths. The person in charge of the records (a Thompson) in the late teens and twenties started a listing of those buried in the cemetery that died as a result of an accident. Let me list some of them for you, out of a total of about ninety-five entries. The last entry is for 1945, and there are several prior to 1913, when the first dated entry occurs. I have often wondered if this is the only place these early accidental deaths were recorded. If so, it is very sad that the end of a life would only be shown in the following fashion:

> Dogemant –French – suicide
> Unknown Man – killed by train
> Decobert – French – murdered
> Wm. McCombs – Scalded by Lewis Lye
> Leur – French – murdered
> Won't use name – killed by fall, while drunk
> Unknown Infant – Found Dead
> Margaret Gray – burned by gasoline stove
> Sick girl – killed by horse
> Man – killed Mar, 1916, Wilford Saloon
> Davis Boy – shot accidentally
> Man – killed Mar, 1915, Wilford Saloon
> Man – Shot by State Police

Most of the others are mine accidents, train accidents, suicides and drownings. After 1945 accidental deaths are not listed separately. There is also a list of soldiers buried in the cemetery. This was probably done to ensure that a flag decorated each military grave on Decoration Day. For many years this was another obligation assumed by the Thompson family, but more recently the local American Legion Post has taken care of it.

Chapter 7

The Great Depression and World War II

We left McHugh Funeral Homes operating in two locations, Shelburn and Hymera in the 1920s. In those days the business realized some growth, but most calls were from the two towns and the area between them.

If we begin the 1930s in October, 1929, events of great interest to McHugh Funeral Homes began to occur with regularity. First of all was my birth on October 11, 1929. This was about two weeks prior to Black Friday, the crash of the Stock Market, and the birth of the Great Depression. There were almost no businesses in the United States that remained unaffected by these tragic times, and McHugh Funeral Homes was no exception. If consumers and laboring people have no jobs or money, then business owners suffer with them. My grandfather and father found themselves trading funerals for livestock, guns, or anything of value the family of the deceased might be able to spare. Many funerals were purchased on credit, since they were a necessity and in many cases there was no money available. I can remember my father saying he had several years in the 1940s when he received more on old accounts than he did on the current year's business.

To most people, although not all, a funeral was a debt of honor. Once late in my career a man from Michigan came into my office and asked me to look up the funeral of his brother who had died in infancy in the 1920s. I located the account, which was unpaid. The gentleman said his mother had made him promise on her deathbed that he would come to Shelburn and pay the account. He asked about interest, and I told him that anyone who would pay a debt well over fifty years old should not be charged interest.

Many people paid their accounts off over time. I remember one older lady of modest means who lost a son in a logging accident. At the time of the arrangements she asked if she could pay the account with monthly payments. We agreed on an amount and she went for quite a period of time without missing a payment. Then one month she missed coming in. The next month she was back and asked if she could just make one payment. When I told her that was fine she said she couldn't make all her payments that month and she was sure I would complain the least. It was the only payment she ever missed.

Not all clients were that reliable. We would have several thousand dollars unpaid each year. Once in a while I would get concerned and try to be more business-like in making arrangements. By the time I was in charge and my grandfather and father both deceased, many families had life insurance on their loved ones. In the early years in most rural locations, life insurance premiums were collected by what was called a debit agent.

This representative of the issuing insurance company called monthly or weekly on those families who held insurance policies mostly designed to cover funeral expenses. The premium was usually as low as five or ten cents a week, and in most cases was saved in a calendar with a pouch on the back and kept on the reverse side of the kitchen door. Payments were made on each of the policies owned, in most instances on the parents and each of the children. The agent called at the same time and day that the premium was due.

Life insurance was carried by many people but certainly not by everyone. When it was not in force or in too small an amount I would sometimes request a promissory note be signed for the amount owed on a funeral. Many of them would not, and it was most usual when there were four or five adult children paying for their last parent. If you managed to get each of them to sign for their percentage of funeral expenses, invariably one of two would fail to keep up with their part and those still paying would insist they only owed for their percentage. The idea was to make each child jointly and severalty responsible, but you couldn't explain that principal to their satisfaction when it was their sibling's share. When I finally sold out, I was able to charge off $55,000 in bad debts in addition to the amount I had charged off each year.

We never brought suit against anyone. It would not have looked good to sue a widow with several children who had lost her husband. I tried collection agencies, but the ones I dealt with turned the account and the expense over to you when it came time to go to court. They also charged a high percentage of any payments they did collect on your behalf. I remember one case where this guy lived pretty well. His wife passed away and he assured me he would pay off the balance after he gave me the proceeds of a small insurance policy he had collected at her death. The balance of about six hundred dollars remained unpaid for many months with no word from him. Finally I heard that he had moved to another state. One day I saw him go by the funeral home, and I jumped in my car and followed him to the American Legion Post. I copied his license number and went into the bar, where the guy bought me a beer and told me things were going fine for him, and he would send me a check when he got home. The results of this promise were the same as the previous ones, so I secured the address from the license number I had copied, located an attorney in the city where he lived and asked if I had much of a chance with a lawsuit. The attorney said I had two chances: little and none. I asked him what he would charge to really harass the guy legally. He quoted a figure of sixty-seven dollars (remember we are talking about a long time ago!) I sent the sixty-seven dollars, but all I got was the hope he had suffered some inconvenience. I want to stress you only remember the accounts you had trouble with, and that most people paid in full in the manner agreed upon.

We're back in the 1930s, however, and we're discussing how the Great Depression affected the business. An examination of the records indicated funeral costs did not increase much in this period. Life insurance was more in evidence and company, union and government benefits applied in more cases. McHugh Funeral Homes continued to have some increase in the number of funerals provided.

In 1934, a two-story home on the state highway in Hymera caught fire. Even as it still burned my father visualized it as a funeral home. It was just one block north of where we were located, would be a great improvement, and would give

McHugh Funeral Home, Hymera, Indiana. Frame part purchased and rebuilt in 1934. Brick section added years later.

McHugh Funeral Home, Shelburn, Indiana.
Constructed in 1935-36. Still in use.

the business much more exposure. My grandfather and father were able to purchase the property and rebuild it as a funeral home. The living quarters in the funeral home were much nicer than the home we were in. One thing didn't work out for me since my mother could see the playground at the local elementary school, where the playground equipment included wooden seesaws or teeter-totters. She impressed on me to not use this equipment due to the possibility of splinters. I was in the first grade and ignored the order. The splinter was large and deeply-imbedded into my you-know-what. I refused to admit the presence of the splinter and it was diagnosed by my sitting in school on one side. When finally acknowledged, a doctor had to cut the splinter from a huge swollen, infected lesion. I stopped using the seesaw.

When the new funeral home was completed, it had glass chandeliers in the chapel, double doors for removing the casket after a funeral, a two-car garage and a floor to ceiling backdrop at the front of the chapel which served as a backdrop for the casket. Not everything was great, however. There were no architects in our area knowledgeable about funeral home design and some choices were humdingers. There were two small rooms behind the backdrop. One was made into the preparation or embalming room and the other smaller one became the rest room for the public. Can you imagine the inconvenience and embarrassment caused by these locations? There was also a display room for caskets upstairs that could only be reached by a very steep and narrow stairway. There was no parking except along the narrow shoulder of the highway. Seating for the family at funerals was in our dining room, unless it was a large enough family to also need the living room. Despite these and other shortcomings, both the funeral directors and residents of the town were proud of the new facility.

I am pleased to report the fact that in 1935, my grandfather and father began construction of a two story building in Shelburn, which was the first building in a very wide area ever constructed for the express purpose of serving as a funeral home. The building included some nice improvements such as larger size and a rope-operated elevator to lower caskets from the display room upstairs. But would you believe that the preparation room and the public restroom sat on each side of the elevator and all three were behind the casket display drape! Not only did the arrangement continue the inconvenience of the Hymera Funeral Home as to the location of the preparation room and restroom, it added to the inconvenience by locating the piano provided to accompany singers next to the space where the rope elevator reached the lower floor. Any musicians participating in a service had the choice of stepping directly to the front of the chapel, through the casket backdrop to the music location, or they could go outside the funeral home around the building and enter this area through a door up about six steps to line it up with the flower van parked there to receive the flowers at the end of the service. Neither arrangement was very satisfactory. Since my mother played piano and sang on many of the funerals, she was able to lead the musicians to their proper place.

By this time we were making funeral arrangements with all families at the Shelburn funeral home. We always offered to pick up the families and bring them there, but almost all of them preferred to drive there. Remember the communities were close together and families could meet at the funeral home as well as anywhere. It was better for us to meet there due to the elevator which was designed to lower the casket from the display room to the ground floor. All of this sounds much better, but can you imagine that after two years of experience in the new Hymera building they had still placed the public rest room on one side of the new elevator and the preparation room on the other with all three behind the display drapes. They had added an exit behind the elevator, so that it was barely possible to bring a cot in that way in case of a death while we were already busy. You could also bring in a casket that way but it was a tough job. I'm not intending to be critical of these decisions, since they were made only as a part of dealing with a new idea, a funeral home from scratch. There was no place to see what others had done, and no one was an expert.

A number of years after this, some friends of ours from the next town east of Hymera came to look our Shelburn location over prior to building a new funeral home and corrected some of the more obvious mistakes.

My Grandmother McHugh had passed away in the early30s, and my grandfather married a lovely widowed lady, who was the only grandmother I ever knew. They moved into the new funeral home in late April 1936. In the first week of May 1936, my grandfather made the annual pilgrimage to our Indiana Funeral Directors Association Convention in Indianapolis. Since U.S. 40 was being constructed southwest from Indianapolis, my grandfather returned on U.S. 36, which was a hilly route with plenty of curves. On the last curve in the road where it came south to enter Clinton a truck crowded him off the road and the car turned over. He lived for a few days but died in time to have his funeral in the barely completed new funeral home. This was an unusual enough event to have people old enough to remember to still speak of it. A man works most of his life with his son to build a new building for their funeral business only to have his funeral the first one in the building. My grandfather and father had been able to pay for the new building with the cash from selling some stock they had accumulated over the years. The cost of the building had been ten or twelve thousand dollars, which would buy a lot of building in 1936. I have always wondered about this decision to sell the stock of some Fortune 500 companies to pay cash for the new funeral home. Twelve thousand dollars' worth of stock in 1936—what might it have been worth today? There is at least a chance it would have been worth far more than our business

My father had some hard decisions to make, due to his father's death. He decided to move his family into the Shelburn Funeral Home, and hire someone to assist in operating the Hymera location, since there were normally more funerals in Shelburn as it was a slightly larger town. The first man who worked for us there was very good and remained for nearly twenty years. Another occurrence during the depression years was a mass movement of people from the area of our county to the automobile towns of Detroit, Flint, and Pontiac, Michigan. So many left our area of Indiana that in later years they and their children and grandchildren used to hold Sullivan County reunions in Pontiac which were attended by several thousand people. The first generation that made this exodus for the most part would return to Indiana for their funeral and burial. By the time their deaths began to occur I was old enough to accompany my father on these trips and they lasted long enough that I took my children on some of them.

My grandfather and father took the position that you could make this trip very reasonably, since if you had a Michigan firm receive the body, take care of the paper work, and perform the embalming, you could go after the remains with a cot and have the family make funeral arrangements and purchase the funeral on our end of the trip. We were very successful in this arrangement, and I remember one year I made the trip ten times. Usually we would drive both ways without sleep, although that sometime caused some narrow escapes for the driver when they became too sleepy. I can remember driving with the windows open in cold weather, stopping along the side of the road for rest, and buying cold drinks and sandwiches I didn't want just to keep awake. After a number of years, the next generation of those who had moved no longer left Michigan at the time of death, but had services and burial there, as they considered themselves Michiganders.

In the early years of World War II another great exodus went from our community to the huge plants in the Detroit area. The companies there were desperate for workers to help in the construction of the tanks, armored cars and other land based vehicles so necessary for the war effort. Among the thousands who joined the journey was my mother's dad who had joined our family circle after his wife died in the early thirties. Like most of the others who headed for Michigan, he found an excellent job with high pay and a nice place to live. It appeared that he was going to change his lifestyle, but within a few months of his arrival the Detroit race riots came upon the scene, and he headed back for Shelburn on the first available transit and would never believe that the riots had completely ended. Many of his friends went back for the good jobs and high salaries but he was satisfied with mowing the grass at the funeral home and setting up the equipment for burial services.

It worked for him too; he died at 86 from complications after a broken hip. He was in the hospital several weeks prior to his death, and I slipped him in a beer and a cigarette several times. I can never remember him giving me a cross word in my life. He was a well-liked gentleman who would have been a good addition to the staff of the funeral home, but he wanted no part of it. The desire to be no part of a funeral home must have run on my mother's side of the house, since none of our three children ever considered it, or at least not for very long, my sister studied accounting in college and became a school teacher, marrying a serviceman early in the war and moving to Cape May, New Jersey, to be with him during his tour there. We made two or three wonderful visits there. It was at that time a historic sea resort with huge homes and hotels along the beach. It was my first opportunity to do any ocean swimming and I loved it. At about fifteen years of age I thought I could stay in the water when the alarm was sounded to vacate the beach. After once or twice I decided the alarm was sounded for a reason. We visited Atlantic City and New York while on these trips to see my sister and her husband. It worked out that we were in New York and Times Square on VE night, the end of the war in Europe and still considered one of the largest celebrations ever in the Big Apple. There I was in one of the wildest times ever in New York with my mother. It was by far the most people I ever saw at one time. One of the most famous pictures to come out of World War II was of a sailor giving a young lady the biggest embrace and kiss you can imagine. Just as most of the other two million people in the streets, I felt that I had seen this famous one, but realistically it was not the only kiss, just the most famous one.

After my father moved into the funeral home in Shelburn, he became active in community and church matters there and grew to be a man many in the town contacted to discuss their problems and seek his advice, sometimes on very personal matters. Once, a single lady of the town came to him seeking advice regarding abortion. He learned the name of someone who would perform the service from a doctor friend and told the lady where to go and who to contact. Abortion was not as well accepted as it is today. He saw the lady several weeks later and asked how everything had worked out, when she told him she was having trouble raising the money to pay for the service, my father told her to contact the father and perhaps he might help. When he saw her again, he asked if things had gone well, and she said, "I'd say it did, I contacted them all, and made twenty-five dollars extra on the deal!"

On another accession, a miner announced to his friends he was marrying a lady from Farmersburg. All of his fellow workers told him she had been in the company of every eligible man up in Farmersburg; he replied, "Farmersburg is a small town." Most of those who sought his advice or assistance had less interesting but no less important issues concerning them. Many were financial problems or problems with spouses or children. Usually he could hear them out and give them suggestions that might help them.

In the meantime, I was growing up and helping on ambulance work and on funerals. I wanted no part of the embalming room or the work that went on there at that time. Upon graduation from high school, I went through Indiana State University on a Business Administration/Accounting major, with little or no interest in joining in the family business. I was graduated from college in June 1951 and drafted into the U.S. Army in August of that year. I was very lucky to be selected for counterintelligence training rather than going directly to Korea. I proposed marriage to my girlfriend, and upon acceptance we were married and went to Baltimore, Maryland, for my training. I served the balance of my service time in Kentucky, and was discharged in August 1953. In the meantime I had told my father I would go to Mortuary School, and try the funeral business for two years. I was already the father of my first son and the security of the established funeral business had more appeal.

By the time I had completed Mortuary School, we had two sons, so we moved into a home in Shelburn and I went to work for McHugh Funeral Homes. During this time my father had become embroiled in an investigation with the Internal Revenue Service. My father never really recovered from the intensity of this investigation, and he never told me what it cost him, but it was plenty. There was never any doubt of his guilt, but I was told by a good friend in the IRS at that time that many cases of similar nature were not treated that seriously, and that he thought the agents in charge of his case were trying to make themselves a name. Both of the agents came to me later and told me they had never checked on anyone who was held in higher regard than my father was in his community.

I need to recognize some ladies who were instrumental in the operation of McHugh Funeral Homes. First of all, my mother and my wife: both served without pay and each did the cleaning or supervised the cleaning of the funeral home in which they lived. In addition they did at least their share in the

24/7 answering of the telephone; they attended the door during visitation if my father or I were unavailable due to ambulance or other duties. My mother also sang for funerals with a friend many times. Each of them would on occasion drive in funeral processions or take patients who could be transported in cars to doctor's offices of hospitals. I remember once when my mother entered the casket display room and increased the price of each casket, which at that time included the total cost of the funeral, by one hundred dollars. My father, when he realized what had happened, decided to leave things alone, feeling my mother probably knew what she was doing.

I told my wife when we married that I would keep the embalming room clean and she would never have to enter it. I think she only did so twice. Once a good friend of my father's from Terre Haute who was a coal miner stopped in to view the remains of a friend. My wife told him that his body was not in the casket yet, was still on the table and not suitable for viewing. The gentleman told her that my father knew they were both coalminers and allowed him to go into the embalming room if this was the only time he could come. Imagine my wife's surprise when she opened the door, which she had almost never done, only to discover there was no body on the table! The explanation was simple; when she heard it later, but turning back to the potential visitor and telling him there was no remains present was something she never forgot. My father and I had taken the body of the man's friend to the other funeral home for preparation, since at the time of his death there was another body on the embalming table at the location where the man had called.

The only other time my wife entered the preparation room, a family came to the door and no one else was there.

This family told her that their father had died from an apparent heart attack on the street in a nearby town and had been brought to our funeral home. They told her that their father always carried fifteen hundred dollars attached with a safety pin to his undershirt, and they would appreciate her giving it to them. My wife thought about asking them to return when my father or I were present, but she thought this might not sound too good, so she asked them to be seated, went into the Prep room where their father's remains laid on the table fully dressed. She unbuttoned his shirt and examined the undershirt thoroughly, finding neither money nor safety pin. Feeling a little distraught, she returned to tell the man's family there was no fifteen hundred dollars. She could only imagine what they felt had happened. Later that day the state police, who had been at the scene of the death, returned the fifteen hundred dollars to the family, relieving them as well as my wife.

All of the wives of the employees who worked for us over the years were expected to assist in the same fashion my mother and wife did at the funeral home where their husbands worked. They were not paid either, as this was the accepted arrangement in the funeral business at this time. Their apartment, of course, was rent-free, but that wouldn't have approached the value of the time they worked to help their husbands and us.

Several other ladies were invaluable to us. Almost every family wanted a hairdresser to attend their deceased family member. In the case of men who died, we could shave their beard and trim their hair. (You didn't have to do the back of the head.) I once buried a barber whose son was also a barber. When the son came with his mother and siblings to arrange his father's funeral he brought a set of electric clippers to trim his father's hair. His father had died from cancer and been in the hospital several weeks and his hair was about as long as it could be. I had already removed the longest hair and, I felt the clippers might be a good idea since the entire family was concerned with his hair looking nice. There was only one thing wrong. The clippers that I thought would only trim a portion of the hair evenly were those that removed the hair to the skin. Fortunately I started on the left side of the barber's head, but with two strokes I had shaved his sideburn completely away. The son and the other members of the family were very considerate when I explained what had happened. I had also glued some hair back where the sideburns had been, but they were much nicer about the mistake than I deserved.

In regard to needing assistance from outside ladies, one of the most important was a beauty operator. Often the regular hairdresser of the deceased would handle this but many preferred not to do so. A lady named Margaret Wells began to arrange the hair of those whose personal operator chose not to come. She began to help my father in this manner in 1942. To illustrate the loyalty of those in small towns, Mrs. Wells is still performing this service for the current owners, and she has certainly never been overpaid.

For many years, I had some sisters from Hymera who helped with the spring-cleaning of the funeral homes and my residence after we moved from the funeral home. The crew usually consisted of whoever was managing the funeral home being cleaned, myself, the wife at the location being cleaned and two or three of these sisters. With this size crew and a little planning we could accomplish a lot in one day. Each of the funeral homes was a two-story building. We cleaned the walls, ceilings, and carpets or flooring in every room, drapes, windows, furniture, folding chairs, caskets, and all equipment. We used steel wool and gasoline to remove the wax from hardwood floors. We could usually clean one funeral home per day with another day for our residence. When we had three funeral homes, this made for a very full week. These sisters worked so hard that the men could not keep up with them, although I exhausted myself trying. Better cleaning material, professional cleaning firms and cleaners have outmoded most cleaning of that type, but I sure wish they had arrived on the scene earlier. The cleaning schedule was always subject to revision should a death call arise at one of the funeral homes. An already complex plan became even more so, as we attempted to take care of the business that arose while cleaning was in progress. About as hectic a day as we ever put in was once when we were redecorating the Shelburn Funeral Home. We received a call during the night prior to the day we were to complete the redecorating. Through the cooperation of the contractors working for us and the efforts of our employees and ourselves on that day we plastered the ceiling of the chapel, painted the walls, cleaned the remainder of the room, sold the funeral, dressed the deceased, put everything back together and had visitation that evening in the chapel. It exhausts me just to remember that day.

We were also well served by another group of ladies that many of you have never heard of or remember. Prior to automatic telephone exchanges, each community had telephone operators who connected parties on the exchange by plugging connectors from one phone line to another. If my father and mother or later my wife and I were going to spend an evening at a friend's house or at another location with a phone, we just advised the operator and she would switch our calls to the

number where we were. That must have been the "call for-
warding" of those days. For this extremely valuable service,
we gave each of the operators a box of candy at Christmas.
Talk about big spenders! Later on when local telephone companies had better service and equipment and more variable
services, we had it set up so that in one community the man-
ager of the telephone company office, who had this exchange
in his home, could answer our number at his home. In Shelburn, I had an extension of our phone in the residence of a
blind man who lived with his parents. He was thrilled at the
opportunity to have some responsibility and would not even
go to bed in fear of not hearing the phone if he was on duty.
We paid each of these answering services something for their
time, although I can't remember the amount.

For quite a number of years prior to selling the business, I
had direct lines between two of the funeral homes, so that we
could answer for both places. As I sit here over twenty years
after selling out, the boxes that allowed the systems are still
located at the edge of the desk in my house where I am working. All of these things seem ancient in view of today's communication systems, but they were very meaningful improvements to us at that time.

I also purchased what I think must have been the first
portable radio-telephone unit. It allowed me to answer the
phone three hundred feet away at the portable unit. I recall
roofing the Shelburn Funeral home with the unit up there with
me. I could also go fishing on a small boat I had for the lake in
the field next to the house we built when we moved from the
funeral home but were still in business.

It is difficult to explain how confining the ambu-
lance/funeral service was. For several years we were covering

three towns approximately five miles from each other constantly. We were usually doing this with six people when everyone and their wife was on the job, but with fewer when we were gone on business or someone was off or on vacation. It was an important part of the job. Beepers came along, and we learned to use them to allow ourselves a little more freedom. I drove the ambulance to places I wanted or needed to be, and whoever was on the phone could beep me with me calling back for the message. I took the ambulance with me to the parts store in which I was a partner, once or twice to the golf course, and even picked up my wife for dates prior to our marriage. This would cause quite a stir in her neighborhood. I remember once when I lost the beeper on the golf course. After giving it some thought I called the number of the beeper, got some friends to help me walk the course and located the beeper rather quickly. I can only imagine what today's communication has done for ambulance and funeral businesses.

In the 1940s our business continued to grow and prices increased in the normal fashion. Payments from sources other than the family were growing in frequency and amount. There was a VA allowance of $150, a Social Security Death benefit of $255 and an Indiana Soldiers' benefit of $100. All three of these government benefits have stayed the same amount for many years. I always thought it was because no one lobbied for death benefits. Local Union and company benefits could also be available. Insurance proceeds were becoming normal, although they were still designed mainly for paying funeral services and there very few tax or retirement benefits considered in the planning.

In 1949, an event that will never be forgotten occurred in Shelburn. On May 21, a tornado struck the town a terrible blow. Ten people died either instantly or within ten or twelve hours. One other man died a week later from his injuries making a total of eleven victims of the storm. There were about sixty-five people treated for injuries at our local hospital, although many left when they saw others worse off than they were. At the time of the storm, my mother was at her hairdresser's in an area hit by the storm. Our local state policeman came to tell us she was all right and my father said he would go check on her and for me to get the ambulance and go to the hardest hit part of town. At the first place I stopped, the mother of a good friend of mine was lodged in the roof of the house next door to where they had lived. The only thing left of their house was the front steps. I decided that it was going to take a long time to get the lady off the roof, so I went to the next house south or what was left of it. Other people had located the older couple that lived there and felt they needed attention. The lady had head injuries, so I placed her on the cot and sat her husband in the front seat with me. Because of the already dense traffic of sightseers I decided to take the gravel road to Sullivan and the hospital. The injured man next to me never uttered a sound as I sped to the hospital, and I learned later he had six broken ribs among other injuries. He and his wife both survived. When I left them at the hospital, I discovered I could hardly move up U.S. 41 to Shelburn due to the terrible traffic, even though I had a red light and siren. I learned later that other ambulances had arrived and many people in cars took injured people to the hospital. One man with a flatbed truck took over twenty in one trip. I also heard of drivers who refused to take anyone for fear of getting blood in their car.

Restricting our story to funerals and burials, each of the ten immediate fatalities was related to one of the others, so we had only five funerals for the first ten victims. We also sent each of the deceased to another funeral home for embalming; with a request they return them to us the next day. My father and I (I was nineteen) made funeral arrangements with survivors and we had a visitation service for eight of the casketed remains in our one chapel. Hundreds marched through the next afternoon and evening. The other two victims, a man and his daughter, were removed to the man's parent's house for their service. None of the other funeral homes charged us for their services. My father made arrangements to get eight caskets very similar in appearance and quality so that the charges were low and equal for all the funerals. We had some unusual things done for us. One man came into the funeral home with a dozen flashlights and a case of batteries. Another funeral director brought eight cases of embalming fluid from thirty-five miles away. That would have been enough fluid for over two hundred dead, but the man meant well and was not sure of the number of deaths.

As I mentioned, we had five funerals for the ten fatalities. Each of the funerals was in a church and each at a different time on the same day so those desiring could attend more than one funeral. My father and the man working for us at the time (who had a brother-in-law and a niece among the dead) conducted two of the funerals each, and I handled the other, my first. I had two highly experienced funeral directors as my assistants, but they insisted I be in charge. At that time U.S. 41 separated Little Flock Cemetery into two sections, and one of the two people whose funeral I was conducting was to be buried on each side of the highway. We all went to one tent for the first burial service, and then marched across the highway for the other. We must have made quite a sight to the stopped traffic, as there were around 150 people, several of whom wore bandages or were using canes or crutches.

Shelburn suffered severely, it was estimated over 150 homes were destroyed or badly damaged. As soon as the roads were cleaned up, U.S. 41 traffic was routed through the damaged area of the town with volunteers from the American Legion and other organizations manning stations where transits would leave donations for the community.

A few years before this the first victim of World War II to be returned to our county was from Shelburn and we were in charge of his funeral. Every Legion Post and every other Veterans organization wanted to be a part of this service. Many servicemen were already home and a total of seven boys had died in the war just from Shelburn. My father called all the Veterans organizations together and pointed out to them that this was only the first of many such funerals over several years and each serviceman would be entitled to the same honors. At his suggestion and upon agreement of all concerned, it was decided that the local Legions Post of each returned casualty be in charge of the funeral. The first funeral was still large enough to overflow the largest church in town and the procession to the cemetery in the next town north, West Lawn in Farmersburg, reached for several miles. From the standpoint of the community, this first casualty had received an honorable funeral and repeating it over and over for others just as deserving would not be an impossible burden on the entire county, if each Legion Post in each community was in charge of the funeral of the boys from their town.

All businesses and in fact everyone and everything was affected by World War II. The best estimate on deaths in this greatest of all world conflagrations that I ever came across was 61,000,000 deaths with 20,000,000 of that number being Russian.

On a less overpowering level, McHugh Funeral Homes was affected about the same as everyone else by the war. My father was too old for World War II, and I was too young. My brother-in-law and a couple of cousins were involved, with one cousin suffering serious wounds, which still affect him at 81 years of age. Rationing was a part of everyone's life, but by virtue of our ambulance service and funeral business we had an "A" ration card that applied to gasoline, oil and tires. We were in the same condition as everyone else where food, sugar, shoes and other rationed items were concerned. We put out a victory garden in an area behind a Feed Mill next door, but it burned up in the first heat wave since we had no water supply other than rain.

We supplied space to the community for a large sign listing the names of all men serving the country. A gold star was added next to their name if they were killed. The space where this sign was located was in the center of a lot north of the Shelburn funeral home where several generations of boys and some girls played baseball, basketball, and football for a long, long time. I mentioned, the funeral home was completed in 1936, and I believe young people used this space until we moved away from the funeral home in 1971. Almost no one used the field if we were busy in the funeral home, and I have not noticed much activity there since we moved out. The field had served all of the athletes and would-be athletes in town. The games played there are still discussed by those who took part. During the war there were many battles fought in the same field with lead soldiers, machine guns, tanks and cavalry. We constructed little forts and trenches and destroyed them with firecrackers, rocks and bottles. I guess young boys will always play at war.

The author and his wife in younger years.

Chapter 8

Broader Horizons

McHugh Funeral Home continued limited growth in the 1950s. Almost all families were still selecting what was called a traditional funeral, which consisted of an evening or two of visitation and a funeral now mostly in the funeral home, with a burial vault used to protect the casket underground. Visitation was usually until 10:00 P.M. and the service was mainly in the funeral home. There was usually music of some type as a part of the service. Funerals, as was true of everything else, were increasing in price. It was late in the 1940s that a change took place that relieved the work of the individual funeral business in our part of the country. Vault companies which were also increasing their prices and trying to be a more important part of the industry gathered all of the burial equipment owned by their funeral home clients such as tents, grass cover, lowering devices, which were used to lower the casket into the grave, folding wooden chairs and flower basket stands. In return for supplying the outside containers for all of their customer's business, they agreed to assume the setting up of the burial sites for all funerals without raising their prices. This relieved

their funeral home customers of the task, and in many instances allowed them to reduce the number of their employees. The vault companies also kept the equipment in good
condition and replaced it when it wore out in return for the
monopoly of their customers business mentioned above. Vault
companies did make a charge for setting up when a pine box
was used or for a Sunday or holiday service, but all of these
things were on their way out.

Discussing burial service provided by the vault company
bring to mind two stories. We once had a funeral at the West
Lawn Cemetery at Farmersburg on quite a rainy day. There
was a young lady present in a car quite a distance back from
the hearse who was restricted to a wheel chair. I had not
thought she would come to the tent for the committal, but her
family told me in advance she wanted to come to the tent. In
an effort to keep things moving, as soon as we got to the
cemetery, I told the two young strong vault company employees who were present, to see if they could assist the girl in the
wheel chair. Imagine my horror when I looked back to see
them on each side of the wheel chair pushing her at a run toward the tent. About the time they reached the area of the tent,
the wheel chair hit a small monument and the poor girl was
dumped in the mud. This experience rates as one of the most
embarrassing of my career.

Toward the end of my career, the vault company that set
up the tent and other equipment for committal services for almost all of our services was improving their service by such
things as larger tents, tents with windows in them and finally
with a gas-heated stove that would provide warmth for everyone in the tent. We always warned those in attendance to not
get too close to the heater, but on crowded funerals everyone

did. They later added a circular bar to the heaters to prevent folks getting too close. The only time I actually had anyone affected by the heater was a lady who singed her coat next to the heater. Take a guess as to what she was wearing. That's right, a fur coat, even yet a mink fur coat. After a long time, the insurance company of the vault company paid for the repairs.

Cemeteries had long been against pine boxes, since the weight of the dirt soon caused the box to collapse leaving an unsightly hole and interfering with mowing. The pine boxes used for burials for many years were also used to ship caskets to funeral homes. We stored the boxes in the garage, and my father would sometimes go along with a pretty nice joke on some of my friends when we were kids. We would talk one of my friends into getting into one of the boxes, we would screw down the lid and my father, if he had the time, would come out, help us load the box into the hearse with the kid in the dark inside the box. He would then drive out of the driveway while the rest of us shouted "so long." Although he usually only went around a block or two, I am certain it seemed like forever to the "victim" inside the box.

My sister and I also enjoyed taking friends into the chapel with the lights out to show them around. Either she or I would slip upstairs and scream or moan down the open elevator entrance giving those unsuspecting and already slightly concerned guests a real thrill, which many of them never forgot.

Continuing with the new arrangements with the vault companies, their additional services allowed them to have a little say in the operation of the business. They didn't want to work on bitter cold days or on Sundays and holidays, while most funeral homes preferred to keep funerals on a regular schedule in order to not back up on the number of funerals. In many of the northern parts of the country, all burials are delayed until spring with the funeral home, the vault company or the cemetery providing above ground storage until the thaw.

Until my father entered into an agreement with our vault company, my grandfather on my mother's side set up the burial site equipment for our funerals. This was about all he did in return for living with our family in whatever funeral home we were occupying for over fifty years. He had moved in with us immediately after my Grandmother had passed away. He did some of the mowing and helped a little with maintenance and upkeep, but it was a pretty good deal for him. He also sometimes had his friends in for a card game when our family was out for a rare evening. The card game was always in the chapel and everyone played with their hats on and a cold beer. The game broke up quickly when my mother returned.

Cemetery arrangements have continued to evolve. Today, many cemeteries provide a small chapel for committal services, and then move the casket to the burial space after those attending are dismissed. Many cemeteries have also entered the vault business and an increasing number have opened on-site funeral homes. This "everything in one package" may be the next trend to spread throughout the country. Cemeteries also provide mausoleums for above ground burial as well as provide monuments for traditional burial.

As I mentioned previously most funeral directors in small towns find themselves responsible for locating burial spaces in small family or church cemeteries. Often no written maps are available and locating the proper space can be a problem.

I think I was responsible for digging three graves in my career, when we were unable to locate anyone to take on the job. I remember in one of these I had running water. This came about when I broke a drainage tile at the upper end of the grave just as I was reaching the depth I needed to complete the grave. After thinking it over, I dug a trench at the bottom of the grave, filled it with gravel from a nearby road, and broke another tile at the lower end of the grave so that the water could re-enter the drainage tile. Not many people have running water in their grave.

The other two graves I had opened in the wrong place each were the responsibility of one of the better men who ever worked for me and both happened in the same week. After the second one, I went to see him and I thought I had a reasonable discussion with him about knowing that almost all monuments around our country were at the head of the graves and when facing east the grave for the wife was on the left side. He seemed appreciative of me going over these matters, but he then said, "Dick, do you know your ears get red when you are mad!" So much for being the boss.

Let's take a look at cremation as an alternative to burial. Remember, I sold the business in 1984, so cremation has become much more popular since then and many funeral homes provide crematory service. The ashes, or cremains, are usually returned to the family in an urn, which they can bury in a cemetery space, place in a columbarium in a mausoleum or scatter the cremains, making sure that they stay within the law of the state where the final disposal is being made. The funeral director can advise them on these requirements.

You may not be surprised to find that I have a tale to tell you about one cremation in which we had a part. A friend of my father's came into his office one morning carrying a brown paper sack. He took a seat near my father's desk and placed the sack on the floor. He then told that his Aunt Jane had died in California and the family wished to have her buried in the local cemetery. My father expressed his sympathy and asked how he could help, thinking shipment of the remains would probably be by air and we might arrange for a service and burial on the family plot. He then asked when Aunt Jane had died and was amazed to hear she had been dead for about a month. Remember, we knew almost nothing about cremation at that time. My father asked where the remains were now located and the gentleman pointed at the sack and said, "right there." My father, shocked but not wordless, said he would get a shovel and help bury the cremains as requested.

I think I had three cremations in my career. At that time people were just becoming aware of the practice in southwestern Indiana. I only remember the details about one of the three. On this occasion, the family came in and picked out the best and most expensive casket I had. They then told me they wanted cremation after the service. I tried to explain to them that the higher price on the casket was due to it being designed to provide protection for the body of their father in an underground burial and that these features would be of no value in cremation. They said they wanted the best for their Dad. I completed the arrangements and the folks left. About midnight they called and said they had thought about what I had said and decided to use the lower priced casket I had shown them for the funeral. I told them there was no problem to change caskets. That was the only time I ever put two bodies in the same casket plus the first time I have told it!

World War II is now over. All of the boys are coming home, marrying the girls who have waited for their return. The G.I. Bill grants them funds for college and other benefits.

McHugh Funeral Homes hits its stride. My family has now been living in the funeral home since 1936. My sister was married in 1943, her husband is home from the Navy and they have started a family. Prior to their return from New Jersey where he had been stationed, my father decided to purchase them a small home that was actually next door east from the house where my grandfather had first lived in Shelburn. The house was quite small; it needed rewiring which my father and I did, passing inspection with flying colors. We also dug a full basement under the house without such brilliant success.

We began by carrying the dirt out and filling the backyard, which ran downhill to a tiny creek. This soon grew old, so we borrowed a mule and a coal skid, hauling the dirt out on the skid and dumping in the growing backyard. This worked fine except the mule continually bumped his head on the ground floor of the house regardless of what we did to prevent it; we wrapped the mule's head in rags, we dug our exit from the basement deeper, but nothing kept the mule from bashing his head. We finally returned the mule to its owner with a bloody head and hired a man with a gasoline-powered elevator, which delivered the dirt out to our waiting wheelbarrows. Voila! Success at last.

There was one last problem, however. At the rear of the lot was an outhouse, with which some of you may not be acquainted but were plentiful at that time in Shelburn. Since we were going to put in a bathroom as a part of the remodeling, we decided the pit below the outhouse should be filled with the dirt we were bringing from the basement. We then started dumping the dirt into the pit after burning down the outhouse. It was amazing how much dirt we could put in that pit. We mounded it up and ran over it with a tractor several times. Finally my father decided we had enough dirt in the pit to complete the job. He got a concrete block, carried it to the edge of the pit and threw it in, discovering to his dismay that there wasn't enough dirt to prevent a tremendous splash of dirt and you know what else that went all over him. We laughed about that for the rest of his life.

Upon graduation from high school, I entered Indiana State University in the fall of 1947, and was graduated in the spring of 1951, which was during the Korean Conflict. In August of that year I became the first of the McHugh's to enter the Armed Forces of our country. Upon the completion of sixteen weeks of basic training, I was fortunate to be selected as one of ten members of our company to attend Counter Intelligence School in Baltimore, Maryland. This seemed a perfect time to ask my girlfriend to marry me; she accepted and soon followed me to the city of Fort McHenry. We located a furnished apartment in a third floor flat, where I remember not being able to wash behind my knees, since the sides of the tub were too short to stick my legs over and too tall to stick them out.

All in all, the months in Baltimore were great. We met some great friends that we never saw again. Everyone was impressed by the school and felt it was on par with college. My wife found a job and we spent the first months of married life in a city about five hundred times larger than the one in which we would spend almost all or our lives.

Upon graduation from CIC School, we returned to Indiana for a furlough and then my parents took us to Indianapolis to meet a train east to receive assignment as a Special Agent in the Counter Intelligence Corps, which sounds a great deal more important than it turned out to be. There were a few tears shed at the old Union Station in Indianapolis, since assignment could mean anything from Korea to about anyplace in the U.S. I ALMOST BEAT THEM HOME! I was assigned to the office in Louisville, Kentucky, about 145 miles from home. My wife and I found lodging in Louisville and lived there from about July 1952 until August 1953, which was another one of the happiest periods of our lives. Almost everyone in the office was a parent, and it was nothing for a group of us to get together, put the kids in a playpen or a bathtub, and have some great evenings. No one had any money and no one was trying to impress anyone. We were all in the same boat. I did make friends with the commanding officer and got to play golf with him about every week. Our work was mostly doing background checks on military people who had gotten classified jobs, plus inspecting the security forces at plants, which had classified contracts with the government. We wore civilian clothes and worked in an office in downtown Louisville. Two of our guys were actually receiving a housing allowance to live in their civilian homes. Who was it that said, "War is Hell!"

I was discharged from the Army in August 1953, and I had gained so much weight I had to borrow a uniform from another guy who had lost as much as I had gained. I remember the last night before my discharge I drew KP Duty, which seemed logical, since I had pulled it a great many mornings while back in basic training. My dear mother put me in a neat circumstance at that time. She wrote me a birthday card, in which she suggested the commanding officer might want to do something nice for me since it was my birthday. He did, all right, since I was on KP in the kitchen as usual when the company returned from training he noted how my military experience fell short of my mother's expectations and had everyone sing "Happy Birthday" to me. I heard that song for the rest of the day in the kitchen and for the balance of my tour in Camp Breckenridge.

I should include the details of my marriage and wedding trip, which preceded both the CIC School and the assignment to Louisville. You will remember we decided that the security of the appointment to CIC gave us enough confidence in the future to allow us to enter the permanence of marriage. At the conclusion of basic training, those of us who were heading for Baltimore received a five-day pass. Since we knew this was coming my fiancé and I made plans for a wedding trip to New Orleans, where we stayed in the Roosevelt Hotel and danced to the music of Jan Garber in the Blue Room, which will mean a lot to you old timers.

We didn't leave Camp Breckenridge for a month or so after this five-day Christmas pass. My father and mother brought my wife down to visit me. Our housing there fell short of the Roosevelt Hotel, with rooms in barracks-like buildings, multiple showers and bathroom facilities. My mother, who seldom found fault, remarked, "I wish Harry Truman was sleeping on this damned cot!"

President Truman had desegregated the U.S. Army at just about the time we were drafted, and I met a lot of guys who didn't approve of this, although they had very little choice. I'll tell you for certain that most of the sharpest guys I met in the CIC were African-American. They had to be to be chosen from their basic training companies.

We've talked a lot about what I took it upon myself to call normal funerals in southwestern Indiana during my experience there. In other parts of the country, changes of many kinds were taking place. One of the main changes was the use of cremation as a final disposition of the remains. While cemeteries that operated funeral homes, provided monuments and took care of the final disposal were spreading in California, beginnings of these trends were starting throughout the country, and cremation has been responsible for much of the change.

Current estimates of the use of cremation as a percentage of total funerals are at 30%, with that figure expected to rise to 45% by 2025. Already, cremation accounts for 67.5% of disposition in Hawaii, and over 65% in both Nevada and Washington. Most authorities feel that two factors are the basis of the continued and increasing rate of the practice. The first and most obvious cause is the difference in cost. Cremation, not including a funeral or burial service, is about $1850, according to the Cremation Association of North America. The traditional funeral, with casket, embalming and dressing, visitation and funeral service, but not including burial space, opening and closing the grave, or monument, can be over $8000. The items mentioned above can add large and varying amounts to that figure. While extras such as expensive urns, space in a columbarium for an urn, or the expense of scattering the cremains can add quite a bit to basic cremation, the difference remains enough to affect the decision of many people.

The other influence increasing cremation is a little more cerebral. According to Stephen Penthew, Chairman of the Religious Department at Boston University, and author of the book, "Purified by Fire" factors such as funerals being overwrought and overdone, too traditional, are included in the increased acceptance of cremation, as well as the comforting feeling from communing with nature and a certain spirituality found with disposition through scattering of the cremains.

Cremation is more and more accepted and appears to be the trend of the future.

We must also at least mention some newer and developing methods of service and disposal. In the past few years we have seen freezing of the remains, which was designed to preserve the remains until medical science came up with a cure for the cause of death which took the life of the deceased. The family of Ted Williams made this practice famous. A few people have used this procedure, although I haven't heard of a de-freezing yet occurring. More recently, propulsion into space of the remains of the deceased has offered another choice. It is my understanding that some have chosen this method of disposition, which is claimed by its suppliers as being less expensive than a traditional service and burial. There is also now disposition at the bottom of the sea.

Burial societies have been in existence for quite a long time now in most sections of the country. A society replaces the funeral director and the funeral home, providing legal funerals that tend to be simpler, can include or omit embalming, casket, and burial service. Non-profit burial societies can definitely reduce costs.

My career included a great many of what I called "tough funerals." Operating in small towns made "tough funerals" worse, since most directors were often close friends of those involved in such difficult happenings. I would include, but not limit myself, to a definition of tough funerals as those including multiple deaths in a family, suicides, accidents, murders, and deaths from unknown causes. A better word that tough might be "unexpected." Think about Sudden Infant Death Syndrome (SIDS), where an apparently healthy child is found dead in a crib. Is that not "unexpected" and "tough." All of the others I listed above and admitted was a partial list also meet our requirements. Emotional shock becomes a part of the scene as well as normal loss. While I am not lessening the difficulty of a normal death such as the loss of an 85 or 90-year-old parent or grandparent who has been in a medical institution under care of qualified medical people, that type of death cannot be as easily defended as tough or unexpected as the types of death we have mentioned. I believe most of us would agree that this type of death must be accepted as a part of life and while many would wish a service to recognize a life that had been lived, few would place such an occasion at the level of difficulty of the type of deaths we have been discussing. Regardless of the type of death, hospice organizations, death counselors, burial societies, and funeral directors are all available to those who have undergone the loss.

There are many major decisions that accompany death other than the choice of funeral arrangements we have talked about. In many instances, estate and tax considerations come to the fore. Sometimes custody of children is a factor. In almost all situations, distribution of personal and real property is significant. Professional services from appraisers, attorneys, and others in the legal field become unavoidable. Their services can be invaluable in tax savings, in helping make decisions acceptable to all members of the family, and in meeting the requirements of the law.

I was discharged from the US Army in August 1953. Also in that year a book came out that just about stood the funeral business on its ear. The Book was called "The American Way of Death," and was written by Jessica Mitford known as the "Queen of the Muckrakers." She was an English lady and had previously written some other investigative books with moderate success, but she hit the jackpot with this one.

Mrs. Mitford determined that everything about death and burial in the United States was over done, over priced, over sold, and that the wrongs, excesses, and gouging was universal among all segments of the funeral business, including suppliers, casket manufacturers, cemeteries, vault companies, monument companies and florists. Everyone was guilty as charged. No indictments, no juries, no trials. Just Guilt!

The American public was astounded, shocked, and resentful. They raised such a furor that only nine years later the Federal Trade Commission started an investigation. This organization did such a fantastic job that in only twelve more years new rules and regulations were in place that every business in the funeral industry was forced to abide by these guidelines, on penalty of law. This great accomplishment took only twenty-one years, if your math is poor.

As I have mentioned, prior to the book by Mrs. Mitford and the investigation by the FTC, funerals were sold based solely on the price of the casket selected. That was the price whether one or two nights of visitation were used, this was the price if you used one or four limousines, this was the price if you used fifty or five hundred floral acknowledgement cards, as well as if you used a funeral home or church funeral. The price could be changed by your purchase of one of a selection of burial vaults, or it you needed long distance transportation from either the place of death or to the place of burial.

In the course of their investigation, the Federal Trade Commission conducted hearings at several locations throughout the country. If you were a witness against the funeral business, in most cases, your transportation, hotel expenses, meals, and sometimes your lost wages were reimbursed. On the other hand, if you were testifying on behalf of the funeral industry, you were on your own, buddy!

The new regulations required every funeral home to provide a price list to every family selecting a funeral, or to anyone interested in securing a price list from a number of funeral homes so that prices could be compared. The price lists had to include prices for every service and merchandise offered, such as preparation of the remains of the deceased by bathing, embalming, applying cosmetics and dressing, all needed supplies, an hourly charge for the use of facilities, and a well-displayed price on each casket and vault for sale. Funeral directors were aghast! It might mean the end of the industry as we knew and loved it. As was usual then and remains so today when the federal government gets involved, we learned to live with the regulations. Price lists charged enough for all merchandise and services selected that the cost of funerals ended up being more, much more in a few short years. For a more well know comparison, check the price of medical care over the last twenty-five years.

The industry was so ingenious that dear Mrs. Mitford was writing a new book, entitled "The American Way of Death, Revised" at the time of her death. Incidentally, Mrs. Mitford left instructions that everything about her funeral be elaborate, including great crowds, fine merchandise, large floral displays, and a long procession to a top-line cemetery where an expensive vault and elaborate monument would complete the tribute.

I remember that much was made of the funeral of the casket used for the funeral of General and President Dwight D. Eisenhower. It was a standard military casket that cost $80.00.

However, try to imagine the total cost of a funeral that included lying in state in the nation's capitol with a continual honor guard, a procession down Pennsylvania Avenue, transportation by special train to Abilene, Kansas, with numerous stops along the way, a funeral there for several thousand people, including dignitaries from all over the world, and protection for everyone at the church and cemetery. I am not finding fault with any of this, only that the cost of a casket represents only a small portion of the total cost of the funeral of anyone. Most of you probably remember the pomp and circumstance at the funerals of every world dignitary. Should not anyone deserve the funeral of their or their family's choice? They are paying their own way! I'm leaving this subject to avoid being investigated as a writer!

From the time of my grandfather's death in 1936, we had at least one man working for us. At that time and until the end of my career, Indiana law required that, if you had a building you called a funeral home, you had to have a licensed funeral director assigned to that location. So there were always one or more licensed men on our staff, since both my father and I worked in Shelburn. After my father's death in 1967, I had two licensed men, since I had three locations after 1964. I mentioned that the wives of the employees, just as my wife, worked many hours covering the phone and the door and doing most of the cleaning.

Because I needed at least two licensed men I spent quite a bit of time interviewing and hiring a wide variety of people. I remember one young man came for an interview wearing a sidearm. He had already visited the location at Farmersburg where the former owner had kept a dog park for his bird dog.

He thought this would be a fine home for his attack dog. The guy didn't know me but he had two and a half strikes on him before he reached the front door, most of the time you could check on applicants through former employers or competitors of former employers.

Many applicants looked forward to driving the ambulance wide open on wreck calls, some were very interested in embalming and the restoration of persons killed by disfiguring disease or by accidents; some had heard of the great hunting and fishing in our area. My main concern was finding couples that would like the community and would appeal to the people living in the area. Sometimes you went short-handed for several months. For these occasions and when we were covered up, I had some pretty nice guys in each of the communities that would help me out on ambulance calls or funerals.

One, who was retired as a federal employee earned social security retirement from working for me. I would hesitate to guess how many men over my career told me they worked for or helped my grandfather or father. If someone ever helped unload a casket or gave you a lift on an ambulance patient or on the body of a deceased person, they never forgot it, and they felt they had been invaluable for that one or two times. I always just said we appreciated all the help we received, and such help was often necessary.

As I have mentioned, we often went on ambulance or death calls by ourselves, and any assistance could be vital. I have carried quite a number of patients, alive or dead by myself from their bed or where they lay to the ambulance or hearse, even if it sometimes meant going down some steps. I don't think I ever dropped anyone, but I felt that I was going to many times.

The price of funerals in the books for the '40s and '50s had not increased as much as I would have thought. Totals ran up to six hundred or eight hundred dollars, but most were still in the three hundred to five hundred dollar range.

And so, we are in the late 1950s, I am out of the army, married with two children and firmly entrenched in the funeral business. In a couple of years we decide that my parents were entitled to leave the funeral home and for us to replace them there. Once again we arranged for the phone to be available in their new residence, and my wife and I moved with our two sons. It was not designed any more than the Hymera place to have a family living there. We had three bedrooms upstairs, a living room, dining room and kitchen downstairs and about half of a basement. The remainder of the building was devoted to the funeral business, with a casket sales display room, storage closets, and a small office filling the north half of the upstairs. Our living and dining room became the second chapel in the event we had two visitation services at the same time. When this happened, we were left with tree bedrooms, the kitchen and the unfinished basement to live in. In 1958 our daughter came along to help fill in the space.

We finally moved from the funeral home in September 1971, at which time our oldest son was leaving for college, his brother was a sophomore in high school, and their sister was in the eighth grade. I think everything happened to us in that building that could have. Let me tell you a little about living in a funeral home, at least one designed as poorly as ours.

When we weren't busy, the chapel became a great place for football and basketball games. Tricycles and small wagons worked well there, and later small bicycles. The folding chairs could be used for busses, forts or caves. The elevator opening was taboo, but there was a door through there that led to a small loading dock which was used for loading flowers that made a great jumping off pad. There was a concrete sidewalk connected to a blacktop driveway that together circumvented the funeral home. Bicycles, tricycles, wagons, pedal cars, trucks and tractors used it 1,344,687 times to drive around the building. I know because I counted that many times. Most of the time the persons, whether they were cops or robbers, cowboys or Indians, or US or foreign soldiers, were being shot at by those trailing them. I remember one tractor, which had a clacker, attached to the drive system to represent a motor noise. Ole Dad (me) removed that noisemaker near the end of the 200,000th lap.

We had a few dogs that made their home with us over the years. One of them, a ninety-five-pound Weimaraner, would sometimes howl when a train went by one block east of the funeral home. On at least one occasion a mournful howl went up from the basement to the dismay of all of the people attending a funeral. The emblem of the Elks lodge contained a clock set at 11:00 P.M. as a part of their ritual. Once, I happened to notice the clock read 5:30; one of the boys finally advised me he had been seeing how the clock worked. Our yard was headquarters for play for the whole neighborhood. Of course, all football or baseball games were called off in the event we were busy, but they had normally reconvened by the time we returned from the cemetery.

A few years after we moved into the funeral home, I attempted to provide some relief for the kids by enclosing a portion of the basement with a room with vinyl floors, pine walls and insulation in the walls and ceiling. We put a TV and some small furniture down there. It provided some help but it certainly didn't turn out to be sound proof. About the toughest thing for the kids was trudging up stairs to go to bed while visitation was still in progress. It was hot, hot, hot up there since our first air conditioning system was only downstairs and in those days visitations lasted until 10:00 P.M. Also, for most of those years visitors came upstairs to use our bathroom, since no one ever got used to stepping to the front of the chapel. I finally placed a very small uni-sex bathroom on one end of the enclosed front porch and made a chair-storage room out of the restroom up front of the chapel. You get the idea; a funeral home is no place to raise three children, although we continued the effort for over fifteen years.

Our business continued to provide my parents and my family with a respectable living, which depended each year on the number of persons who died in the communities. Not too pleasant to think about but quite true.

Early in the 1960s two events occurred which affected our business and our lives. We were able to make an addition to the Hymera Funeral Home, which gave us a second chapel and a family room. We also could provide a family lounge and two rest rooms. Shortly thereafter we were able to purchase an empty lot for parking, although it was across the highway from our location. These improvements allowed us to have two visitations at once and to have much more seating for funerals. There was even less space outside and the highway was closer to the door. Facilities for the family of the funeral director working for us there were vastly improved.

The other major change was outside the funeral business. My wife and I were able to purchase a going auto parts business in the county seat with her sister and her husband. There were both advantages and disadvantages to this development. I found that I enjoyed the parts business, and I felt that I could contribute to its success by putting some time there. It gave us a nice additional income from the beginning and realized regular growth. That was a good thing; since I had cashed in everything we had except the life insurance on me to come up with the down payment.

On the negative side of the purchase of the parts store, my wife was tied down tighter to the business, since I was gone to help in that business as well as ours. At about this time, my father's health was slipping and he was no longer able to make ambulance runs. It became a regular practice for me to drive the ambulance when I went to the parts store so that I could go on an ambulance or death call directly from there. Our calls came almost exclusively from the northern third of our county; so that it was possible to serve the area equally well from about any point in that portion of the county. We had opportunities to open other parts stores in other communities but never took advantage of them, feeling that we were spread about as thin as we cared to be.

Things ran rather smoothly for a few years and then, in August 1967 my father died. I was thirty-five years of age and had not only lost my father, but also my business partner. He was the backbone of the business, although his health had not allowed him to be in charge so much for several years.

My wife and I were now living in a funeral home with our three children who are approaching their high school years. We are in charge of two other funeral homes in two separate towns and partners in a parts store in a third location. It was necessary for me to reduce my time at the parts store and become again a mostly full –time funeral director. We adjusted pretty well to this, but it took the public a long time to quit asking for my father when they needed service from our business. I can remember telling my wife that people were beginning to ask me if they wanted to borrow chairs. I guess you have to start somewhere.

Things settled down. I didn't feel that I lost much business due to my father's death, but I certainly didn't gain any. My not being able to give as much time to the parts store tied down our sister and brother-in-law more, but we were able to make some nice trips by learning to rely on the help that we had. Our children had reached the age when they were valuable to us in the business, but we never encouraged them to enter the business, and they were never interested.

One day a few years earlier, I had taken the two boys on a so-called hunting trip to a piece of ground my father had owned just east of town. My older son and I were walking along a low long hillside, when we heard my younger son fire his shotgun on the other side of the hill. I rushed over to him and found that he had not killed himself or anything else. It had been a very rainy season and I noticed a rivulet of water running down the small valley on that side of the hill. I looked the area over and thought it might be possible to dam up the small creek at the south end and form a small lake and perhaps put a home on the west side. We had felt for several years that both our children and ourselves were entitled to live part of our years together away from the funeral home. We checked everything out; I bought the ground from my mother and Sister and in 1971 we had the dam constructed and built a seven-room ranch home near the lake. We were on about ten acres of the field, 750 feet from the street and only about three-fourths of a mile from the funeral home. From that time on, we had an employee and family in the funeral home, which gave everyone a little more time off.

Over our last several years in the funeral home, my daughter was always asking for a horse, and I would tell her when we moved out. Within a week after moving in our brand-spanking new home, she said, "Where's my horse?" She had me. I put up a pole barn, enclosed about an acre by fence and proceeded to buy a thirteen-year-old mare that was smarter than all of us. We never got her out of a walk, until after several years my brother-in-law got on her and had her running several gaits, but she still only walked for us.

My oldest son left for college a couple of weeks after we got in the new place and told me later it took him several trips home before he felt comfortable in the new digs. My other son took it in stride and just went on being a regular teenager.

As of this writing, our oldest son is fifty-three years old and has two children, our second son has three children, and our daughter is forty-eight and married. We have never had any trouble with any of our children or any of our five grandchildren. All of them keep in close contact. They are spread from Indianapolis to Ann Arbor, Michigan, and to Tucson, Arizona.

Another major event occurred the same month we moved into the new home. The funeral homes in our county, along with several other neighboring counties, withdrew from the ambulance service business, except for a small portion of our county. The amount of work as compared to the amount paid for the service then made the business unacceptable to most funeral homes, although some remain in it to this day. I compared getting out of the ambulance service to getting out of jail.

The 1970s continued to be a decade of major change for us. In 1974, I had the opportunity to purchase the only funeral home in Farmersburg from the widow of one of the nicest guys ever in the business. She and a nephew had been running this firm for several years, and it was too small to provide a living for both of them. At the time I made the deal, the three funeral homes had been averaging 122 calls a year for ten years, which together wasn't a very large business, but it made a fairly good package in our county. So I'm now the owner of three funeral homes, and a partner in the parts store.

Taking over the third location went very smoothly. It meant having two licensed men, one for each location with me covering Shelburn. Operating three funeral homes in separate towns with three full time employees kept everyone pretty busy, but with the help of the part-time people I mentioned earlier, we managed to have some regular time off and vacations. It was sure a lot more possible in the absence of ambulance work. For a while I had a third licensed man at Shelburn, but when he resigned, I started using a widow at that location and it worked out fine. I only had two ladies over quite a number of years with one of them still working after I sold out. I did have one commitment that gave me some problems to keep up. Prior to my dad's death we had decided that one of us would make the arrangements for all funerals, be at the funeral home when the family first arrived for visitation, make an appearance at all visitations and conduct all funerals. I struggled to meet these obligations for the three locations, but I seldom failed to meet them.

Fidler-McHugh Funeral Home,
purchased from Mrs. Elizabeth Fidler in 1974.

While feeling that I was keeping within my activity level
with operating the three funeral homes, doing what I could to
assist in the parts store, and keeping up our home with the lake
and seven or eight acres of mowing, I received a rude awaken-
ing in August, 1982, when I suffered a heart attack, the details
of which we are going to get into later. I will mention that attending all of the visitations meant sitting for two to four hours
with up to twenty-five or thirty smokers on about 150 evenings a year. (There were still quite a few funerals that held
two nights of visitation even in the '70s and early '80s.) I
really felt I understood what the medical profession meant
when they started talking about the problem of second-hand
smoke.

McHugh Funeral Homes, Inc., was now operating past its seventieth year of operation. All three locations were maintaining the amount of business expected of them, funerals are continuing to increase in price, we're working a lot of hours, and our children are advancing from high school to college. One year we had all three of them in college, the boys were both married and their two wives were also in college. Everyone had successful college careers and found summer jobs and part-time work when it was possible.

I remember one occasion when we purchased a used car for our daughter at the close of her high school years. Our second son was working on a summer job in Illinois. I asked him to drive her car to work one day to see how he felt the car performed. On the way to work he dodged a dog running on the road, got into loose gravel on the road and wrecked the car pretty badly. He was unhurt, went on to work and told me he noticed on his way home that someone else had killed the dog, and so my daughter waited a while longer for her own car. She ended her education later at Indiana University, where she received a degree as an Audiologist. One particularly miserable day over there someone stole the battery from her car. She gave me a call, and I went by the parts store for a battery and advice. The guys told me it was a standard procedure in such thefts to also cut the battery cables, so I took a set of them along. The weather was such that when I lay under the car the slush would melt, and when I arose it would re-freeze. When I finally got everything set, I discovered the extension cable was about six inches short of reaching the starter. I was lucky enough to find a station open about two blocks away that handled cable extensions, and I was able to finish the job. I still remind her of this little chore.

Shelburn Funeral Home as it appears today.

Chapter 9

A Few Complications

Our daughter and youngest was graduated from Indiana University in 1982, which was to be an eventful year for our business, our family, and especially for me. In the spring we bought two weeks of a time-share on Lake of the Ozarks, Missouri. My oldest son and his wife joined us there after we had made the purchase. His wife was and still is an ardent physical activity advocate. She and I jogged quite a bit on the cart paths of the golf course near our condo. I had taken up jogging on a milder scale after my brother-in-law had suffered a heart attack, so I was at least a novice to her expert status. All of the business affairs, the travel, and the jogging came together on the morning of August 6, 1982, when my heart attack hit me. I had three funerals scheduled for that day at the Shelburn location. There was no one living there at the time, so I had spent the night there. I had only one full time employee at that time. After completing the first funeral, I was cleaning up for the next one when I noticed I was a little tired and lay down on a couch. To my surprise, I remained tired and started having cold sweats. I had felt no pain, but my experiences driving an ambulance left me with no doubt that I was experiencing a heart attack. I called my wife, told her to call the one man working and tell him to come to Shelburn prepared to handle two funerals, since I was going to the hospital with myocardial infarction. My diagnosis was correct and McHugh Funeral Homes was entering what was normally its busy time of the year with no skipper at the helm.

As in the manner of many other business owners, I learned that I was not indispensable. We were able to fill the vacancy at the one location. I remained in our local hospital about a week to let my heart rest, which was a popular practice in those days and then took a stress test at the office of a cardiologist on September 6, when I was in for a severe shock. I had still felt no pain, been bored to death by the month off, and expected to walk the tread off the treadmill. At about four and one-half minutes into the test, I had no choice except to tell the doctor that I had had enough. This led to more medication, another month of rest followed by quintuple by-pass surgery at an Indianapolis hospital on October 6. I talked them into letting me go home ten days later, although they were treating me for blood clots in the lungs, and my wife had heard one nurse, who turned out to be prophetic, say I would be back in the hospital in a week. One short story before proceeding, I had been honored by receiving about three hundred cards from friends while in the Indianapolis hospital, about sixty or seventy of which were of the "dirty card" variety. Word spread throughout the hospital about my cards, and I'm pretty sure every nurse in the hospital visited my room to view the cards, particularly the dirty ones.

Then it was home for recovery, where to my dismay, I encountered the most uncomfortable part of the whole experience. I started having pretty severe heart discomfort, was admitted to a hospital in Terre Haute and diagnosed as having blood clots in my lungs and pericarditis (inflammation of the sac that surrounds the heart). It took over a week to get over this, and I still faced the recovery period at home.

In the meantime, my wife and the two men working for us were handling everything quite well. I understood this, of course, was due to my superior supervision and training and advice. I spent the longest two months of my life awaiting an O.K. to go back to work. I fudged a little bit on visitations, but I really stayed away almost as long as I was instructed.

One interesting happening took place when I returned to the bookkeeping part of the operation of the funeral homes. My wife had been handling the records in my absence, along with everything else. She had received a letter from the Internal Revenue Service with a check for $1275. The letter explained that we had paid the withholding and social security taxes for the employees twice for the fall quarter. When I was feeling better, I went over the records, checked with the bank, and found that the taxes had only been paid once. I mailed the check back to the IRS with an explanation that we had only paid the taxes once. This led to several letters back and forth each one containing the check. Finally, I decided the heck with it. I deposited the check in my bank. You can imagine my surprise and frame of mind when a letter came stating I had received a check I wasn't entitled to receive, which should be returned along with interest due from the date of the first correspondence. I went to my CPA and asked his advice as to how I might avoid the interest portion of the deal. He suggested I return the check without the interest and enclose the most vile letter I could compose telling the whole story. The check cleared and a few months later I got a letter stating I would not have to pay the interest. One more thing, my CPA requested a copy of my letter so that he could use it as a guide for other clients with similar experiences. He thought it was a dandy letter.

The story of my heart attack, treatment and recovery would not be complete without admitting that I entered a period of depression in the winter of 1983. I couldn't get along with anyone, had no appetite and was a bear to deal with. I finally got over it without medication, but it was a tough fight. I am now seventy-six years of age, attend the fitness center at our hospital three or four times a week, and jog two and one/half miles on the days I can't attend the center.

I returned full time to work in the early spring of 1983. The business had survived very nicely also. I thanked my wife, gave the employees a small bonus and took over. Talk about appreciation!

By now all of our children had been graduated from college, one son was an attorney, his brother was a mechanical engineer, and our daughter employed as an audiologist. All three were married.

I had incorporated the business several years before mainly for tax purposes. Everything was proceeding very well. I was soon working on several new things in the business. I was preparing price lists required by new Federal Trade Commission rules. It was during the late '70s and early '80s that prepaid and pre-arranged funerals came into widespread use. Unlike most others, I didn't actively solicit either type of arrangement. I didn't want to handle anyone else's money, and I usually recorded the wishes of those contacting me and sent them to our local bank to take care of the financial arrangements. Many times our local banker accepted burial trusts without even telling me. Never the less the paid up funerals I accepted added up to an amount that was considered very valuable when I finally sold out. Remember, this was the beginning of pre-arrangement and I would have been forced into it on a competitive basis had I remained in business.

Chapter 10

After Life

I was still in my early fifties, but I had suffered the heart surgery experience. I had several inquiries about buying the funeral homes and promised one man I knew first chance if I made up my mind to sell. One day while doing the monthly bookkeeping, I started thinking the whole situation over. I could see where we could sell the funeral business on a ten-year contract, do the same thing with my share of the parts store, and have a pretty decent income for those ten years. If I could do this at age fifty-five, we would be pretty well set until we were ready for retirement. I had a retirement plan in place through the corporation and would be eligible for Social Security, and the investments I had made would have ten years to grow before we touched them. As I have mentioned, I was not as keen on the funeral business as either my grandfather or father.

I remember telling my wife we didn't have to work to be able to live as we did. We talked it over and decided to take the plunge. I called the man to whom I had given the first chance to buy, set a price that was probably too low which was accepted and we sold McHugh Funeral Homes. I also sold the right to use the name "McHugh" in the business forever, and I didn't realize the value of the prepaid and pre-arranged funerals on my books. Oh Well! The next time I sell a funeral home, I'll know better.

The value of prepaid funerals became a valuable asset to the funeral home holding the prepaid account. When the practice first began on a large scale, it didn't appeal to me. I didn't want to hold other people's money, and I didn't want to guarantee a funeral price into the distant future. The practices that were set up with bank trusts, life insurance products, bond and stock investing, and self-investing , among other plans soon proved to me how wrong I was.

However, by the time I got out of business, I had many prepaid funerals, a number of which I didn't even know I had. I sent interested folks to our local bank, and they set them up with a bank trust of which I was the beneficiary at the time of the death of the person setting up the trust. If the person contacting me insisted on my taking their money, I did the same thing with it by setting up a bank trust. It finally got to where the bank would set up trusts for those coming to them without even notifying me. I was sometimes surprised to learn of the trust after the sale had been made. These decisions I made about pre-paid funerals were probably the worst I ever made in the business, but there is another old saying "you can't teach an old dog new tricks." Believe me, the young dogs really got involved in this new phase of the business. When I sold out, I got together with the bank and came up with an accurate accounting of prepaid funerals, so I didn't get hurt too much. It was only that I didn't actively seek the business, which, had I done so would have probably increased the amount of prepaids by quite a bit. It did for everyone else.

I had made myself a promise early on to sell by the time I was fifty-five, and I received the down payment and my first check one week after my fifty-sixth birthday. It was on a weekday, and I remember walking down the street in Terre Haute feeling pretty cool. I went to the office of my broker and invested the down payment. When I closed the door the next morning after getting my personal stuff, I told the new people they could call me if they had a desperate situation they couldn't handle. They had very, very few such situations, probably again due to my great training programs and sound advice, or maybe it was because it was not as difficult to run three funeral homes as I had thought. There were two things that bothered me that I hadn't anticipated. I missed seeing the people in the three communities I served on a regular basis. They were wonderful people; some in each town would come to a visitation or funeral of a person it they felt there wouldn't be a good crown at the service.

The other problem I hadn't anticipated. After my wife and I visited Hawaii and St. Thomas Island right after the sale, I returned wondering what I was going to do. After teaching one semester at a local junior college, I took a job in public relations with one of the banks in our community. In about six or seven months, I realized folks were as loyal to their bankers as they had been to their funeral directors. I resigned to save them the trouble of letting me go.

Next I took classes to qualify as an insurance and securities representative and worked for a good company for eleven years. I didn't work very hard and didn't make big money, but

I felt I had done a good job for the customers who had done business with me.

There are a couple of trends that have grown since I left the funeral business that I feel are not to the advantage of the public. One I have mentioned, the rapid and highly competitive growth of pre-need funeral sales. This became nationwide and the competition was more vicious and questionable than it had ever been in normal funeral business. This competition was practically universal with many firms having more people in their pre-need departments than in their regular funeral operations. Many pre-need plans were not advantageous to anyone other than the sales representative and the firm they represented.

The other and newer trend is the formation of huge conglomerates that own hundreds or thousands of funeral homes in the United States and Canada. My three locations are now owned by a firm in Florida, which bought them from the man I sold to.

While I can find some merit in pre-arranged and pre-need funerals if they are handled properly, not all of them are. I cannot see how the formation of the funeral conglomerates is to the advantage of anyone other than themselves. They are becoming monopolies in many communities, and there are some laws against that.

Chapter 11

Further Adventures

That about sums up the history of McHugh Funeral Homes and the story of caring for the dead through most of man's history. I'm sticking Chapter 11 in to let you know a little more about what happened to the Mchughs before we turn to our final chapter with advice about the advantages and disadvantages of pre-arranged and pre-paid funerals.

We're going to begin the remaining story of the McHughs by starting on a very significant date, September 1, 1971. On or near that date several major events took place. Along with most of the counties in our area, we ceased ambulance operations on that date. This was akin to getting out of jail. Twenty-four/seven, 365 days a year, someone was within hearing distance of a telephone. A call could be anything from a death, serious injury, accidental fall, drowning, or anything you could think of. It could be someone wanting to borrow chairs, Or, as it was many times, it was not really a need for an ambulance or hearse. You needed to remember that, there might be nothing at the source of the call. That's how you kept going; it might be nothing. In that case you just went back home and continued normal activities, back to bed or back to work, or back to enjoying a rare day off.

We also moved from the funeral home to a new home about three-quarters of a mile east. We had built a seven-room ranch type home that was popular in those days. One of the seven rooms was an office from which I could operate the funeral homes, since telephone lines from each of the other towns came into this office. There are advantages and disadvantages from operating your business from your home.

The author and his wife.

Our oldest son left for college on about this date, and he admitted he felt for several of his first trips home to the new place it did not seem like home. I guess you can accept a funeral home as a natural place to live if you're there long enough. Rick is now living in Dexter, Michigan, after having been graduated from Wabash College in west central Indiana and from Law School at the University of Michigan. He is 55 years of age. He and his wife, Marsha have a son, 17, and a daughter, 16. Rick works for the National Employment Law Practice Review. He once argued a case before the United States Supreme Court, and we were able to sit behind him during the proceedings. It was pretty neat hearing him arguing with the Justices of the Court.

Our son David was graduated from Rose Hulman University which was recently recognized for the ninth consecutive year as the best engineering school in the country. David is 52 years of age, owns a very successful metal fabricating business in Tucson, Arizona. He and his wife Leeann have two daughters, the older of which is a sophomore at Lewis and Clark College near Portland, Oregon. The second daughter is a junior in high school and they have a son who is in the eighth grade. David and his family have traveled extensively in Europe and Canada. He and his wife once spent five months exploring Alaska. His business has been a success and they live in a 6,000-square-foot home in Tucson.

Our daughter, Lisa, claimed her horse and barn as soon as we moved into the new home. This was the only building I ever built and it is still standing. Lisa is 49 years old and married her husband, Peter Goerner several years ago. They have not been blessed with children. Peter manages a small company called Single Crystal, which is owned by Rolls Royce and is located in Indianapolis, Indiana. Lisa is employed by her Alma Mater, Indiana University, and is working on a doctorate degree in Audiology, her chosen field.

Jinnie and I added a small lake to our new residence, where we placed a small electric boat, and enjoyed many evening cruises, and a great many visits from our children and grandchildren.

As you will remember, I sold my interest in the auto parts store and my ownership of the funeral homes. I was only 56, so I taught at Ivy Tech College at Terre Haute for a year. I then went to work for a bank which had opened a branch in Farmersburg, where I quickly learned that people there were just as loyal to their banker as they were to their funeral directors. I quit before some old friends would have had to fire me.

I then took some training and passed an examination as an insurance and securities salesman and took a job with The New England, as mentioned in the book. I enjoyed this work and wished I had done it all my life. However, the funeral business had been very good to the McHugh family from 1908 until 1984. All three of the communities which we had served were wonderful to us, and with all the changes, my best decision might have been selling out.

In 2006, my wife and children all began urging me to sell our home and the 57 and 1/2 acres attached and move to a smaller home in a location with less yard work, creek bank maintenance and lake care. We finally did that, moving to Sullivan, Indiana, about six miles away, and the county seat of our county. The home we bought is about three blocks from my Golf Club, but new matters took precedence.

Soon after we moved into the new place, my wife began to complain to her doctor of weakness and fatigue. After about a week of living in the new home, she was diagnosed with fourth stage liver cancer, which had spread from her colon. Despite wonderful medical care and everything her children and I could do for her, she died on July 16, 2007. Her cremains lie buried in Little Flock Cemetery, where we had been connected for so many years. At the time of Jinnie's death, the closing sentence of her obituary read, "Jinnie was a loving wife, mother, grandmother, daughter, sister, aunt, cousin and friend." I'll stand by that.

All of my children, grandchildren, family and friends have been very supportive of me. I am trying to become accustomed to a great change in my life, one that will have meaning and pleasure. You are reading the second book that I have written. I have started on a third one. Regardless of how many books my time and ability allow me to complete, I feel that this work along with the relationship I have with my children, grandchildren, family and friends will meet my requirements. Thanks to all.

The author at his wife's gave site.

Chapter 12

And Finally, Advice

We have come a long way with the history of my family business, and a much, much longer way with the story of man's handling of death and disposition of the dead over much of history. I must open this chapter with a statement of my qualifications to be offering advice in this field. I am not an attorney, I am not a minister of God, I am not anything except a retired funeral director and ambulance provider who served the public for about forty years. I got out about the time prepaid funerals were coming in. I had very little experience in cremation, none in freezing of the dead, none in injecting the remains into space, very little with mausoleums, none in suing the survivors of the dead, and very little in settling estates as an executor or administrator. Bearing these shortcomings in mind, I plunge resolutely ahead to tell you what you should do in preparing your own funeral or the funeral of someone you love. A very high percentage of those people arranging funerals from the consumer side spend more time deciding on what clothes they will wear to a funeral they have arranged than on the arranging itself.

Thus they may spend more time selecting the $200 suit or the $150 dress they will wear to this funeral than they did on arranging the funeral itself, although it may cost $5,000 to $15,000 (or up). I find no fault with the selection of any funeral regardless of cost. It is one of the most personal of choices and very few find fault with the services or merchandise they select. My problem is with the lack of time these folks give to the decision. Will they have regrets later? Will they wish they had done things differently? The decision is normally made in at least a relatively short period of time. In the case of many, many people, a funeral is among the top two or three purchases they ever make. Funerals can rate right up there with some automobiles, some homes, most vacations and a lot of medical treatment.

Let's look at the facts of this decision. It is almost certain you will someday arrange a funeral. As we stated above it will almost certainly be for someone you love or for yourself. It might be for your grandparents, parents, a sibling, your child, grandchild, or great-grandchild. It might be under conditions such as an accidental death, or even a suicide or murder. Are you going to be at your best under any of these circumstances? Of course not, no one with normal responses could be. This is not a sign of weakness or lack of intellect; the death of a loved one is heart-rending. You would not be normal if you were not affected by any type of death to your family or your friends.

There is only one way to lessen your response to one of these situations. That is prearrangement and/or prepayment. These broad fields offer many interpretations. A prearrangement can be as simple as telling your spouse or child that you wish to be buried in a certain cemetery or that you want to be buried in your brown suit. It can go as far as listing your wishes, in writing, to members of your family or with a funeral director or attorney or executor of your will. A word of caution, in many states the body of the deceased becomes the personal property of the next of kin. The next of kin should be

Medical Plan

401K Plan

Retirement Plan

aware of your choices and approve of them. A lot of times families have ended up in court cases where there was disagreement as to the plans pre-arranged.

Learn about the rules or laws about pre-arrangement in your state. Talk with an estate attorney, perhaps with the attorney who wrote your will. You do have a will, don't you? An ideal story of a couple pre-arranging their funeral services might go something like the following theoretical situation. Bill and Mary are into their fifties, they have two children who have moved away from where they were raised and have families of their own, giving Bill and Mary four grandchildren who are their greatest loves. Bill has a retirement plan where he works, health benefits, and a small life policy included in his retirement plan. The couple earlier purchased ordinary life insurance policies on each of their lives with a death benefit of $100,000. They have owned a home in an area of their city that has increased in value over the years, so that their home is probably worth $500,000. Let's ignore the possibility of the current negative situations coming up in regard to health and retirement benefits. We will further assume that the insurance company they selected has weathered all the tribulations of the financial services industry. If we add up their 401k plan, their retirement plan, the cash value of their life insurance, the market value of their home and their personal property such as cars, furniture, and savings plans, Bill and Mary would be surprised and pleased to learn their combined estates have a value of about $2,750,000.

Bill and Mary decide that it would be well if they learned as much as they could about funerals, funeral requirements, and funeral customs. They soon discover that the field is much broader than they anticipated. Many religions have certain required practices. If Catholics meet certain requirements their funeral must be in a Catholic Church. Similar requirements must be met to be buried in a Catholic Cemetery.

Jewish people must use a casket without metal parts and funerals are to be held the next day following the death. The Church of Jesus Christ of the Latter Day Saints (Mormons) have three speakers for their services. These are just a few requirements and customs in a very few churches. We could fill another book with them if we chose to do so.

If we stick with Protestant and Catholic practices and add legal requirements we will begin to discover just what a wide field we are considering. All of these requirements formed part of the reasons for the development of the need for a funeral director, who should assist with all of these decisions and requirements. setting the time and place for the visitation and funeral, notifying the media of the times selected, is there to be embalming or no embalming and any requirements in this regard, will cremation be used and if so, will there be a funeral and burial service, or scattering the remains in line with state law, will there be embalming, a complete normal funeral including visitation, a service and burial, contact is to be made with minister or priest, music service if desired by either singers, musicians or recorded equipment, contact with cemetery if one is to be used, a mausoleum, crematory or one of the more exotic forms of disposal, contact with social, fraternal, or civic groups the deceased held memberships in and alerting them if their organization is to be a part of the service, decisions regarding the use of flowers or donations in lieu of flowers, clothing to be used if there is to be visitation, depending on the type of service, a casket must be purchased, an outside container such as a vault, selection of register book for guests, memory cards, acknowledgement cards for flowers, arrangements for flowers from family if desired., if cremation is being used an urn is usually purchased for the cremains, are family cars to be used or those provided by the funeral home, filing and securing certified copies of the death certificate, notification of government benefit programs, company benefit programs such as retirement must be changed to death benefit programs. In addition, there is everything I forgot.

In short, there is a lot to be done, and it grows more involved and complicated as the years go by.

Bill and Mary will need to check with their tax accountant about federal and state inheritance tax. We are here to assist in planning their funeral arrangements; those matters require other expertise. After talking with some friends, the attorney that wrote their wills, and the minister of their church, Bill and Mary decide to pay more attention to obituaries in the newspaper. Instead of sending a card of condolence to friends who have suffered losses to death, they begin to go to visitations, and to funerals at different mortuaries. They talk to those who have gone through such losses, both extended relatives and friends. They decide over a few months to visit three funeral homes in their community. At each place they consult with a funeral director who shows them throughout the establishment, goes over their merchandise and service price lists, explains the lists and answers their question. They like the facilities and the director they meet at the Community Funeral Home. They decide that each of them prefers a traditional funeral with an afternoon and evening for relatives and friends to meet with the surviving spouse and the children and grandchildren. The funeral will be the next morning with their local pastor in charge. Semi-classic organ music will be played for a short time prior to the service and as those attending leave. After they are gone, a few minutes will be set aside for the immediate family to spend with the remains of the deceased. The service will then be concluded by a procession to the cemetery and a short service there.

While in the pre-arranging setting, the funeral director they have chosen has accompanied them to the Maple Crest Cemetery which seemed nice to them. They select and pay for a two-grave burial plot. The cemetery will probably offer them a monument for their lot and a selection of burial vaults for the interment. Bill and Mary decide to delay the selection of these items as they decided to delay the selection of the casket until the first of them passes away so that their children can take part in that portion of the arrangements. All of their pre-arrangements are written out and they get copies of everything, including receipts for the selection of their cemetery lots. Bill and Mary place one of their copies in their lock box at the bank and the other in a desk at their home. In most states, a lock box can only be opened in the company of a representative of the County Assessor's office, and the death might be on a weekend.

Bill and Mary go over everything, discuss their plans with their children, their attorney, their pastor and their accountant. They are comfortable and pleased with their plans, as they should be, since very few couples actually complete such pre-arrangement agreements.

As they are leaving, the funeral director with whom they have met hands them a small brochure designed to explain the practice of pre-paying which has become very popular throughout most of the United States. One of the reasons for this is the tremendous advantage to the funeral home, which sells the pre-payment plan. In the past several years many fu-neral homes have had more people selling pre-payment plans than they had arranging and conducting funerals. A pre-arranged, prepaid funeral is listed among the assets of the firm and a large amount of such assets adds to the value of the fu-neral home in the event it is sold. Bill and Mary feel that they should check out prepaid funerals, since there are several ad-vantages also to those purchasing a prepaid service.

First of all, with such a plan, Bill and Mary have secured the funeral they have selected at the price at the time they made the prepayment. If the funeral home they use invests the money they deposit in their plan so that it has more value at the time of their death, the profit goes to the funeral home. However, if the plan is worth less at the time of their death, they still get the funeral they selected. The funeral home pre-sents their statement to the institution holding the money at their current price. If the plan has grown, they receive their price plus the gain; if it is less Bill and Mary still get the fu-neral merchandise and services they selected.

The funeral home many times invests the money in an insurance policy on the lives of those participating in the plan. The growth of the cash value within the plan is intended to allow for inflation and possible growth. Many other prepaid plans are made through Bank Trusts, where the money in the plan is placed with a bank, and the interest it earns is to keep up with inflation and perhaps some extra gain. There are even firms who invest prepaid funeral trusts in a blend of guaran-teed investments such as bonds, annuities, and investments that are sure to raise in value, along with investments in com-mon stocks and mutual funds that can go up or down. Some funeral homes invest their prepaid plans themselves, feeling that they can meet the requirements of the plan regardless of the results of their investments.

We must mention that all these plans must be irrevocable. That means you can't change the plan once it is in effect. The reason for this is that in the event of financial losses on the parts of Bill and Mary or on the funeral home, the plan stands alone in the eyes of Medicaid, which is the institution that would pay either Bill or Mary's expenses in a nursing home should they lose their considerable holdings through financial misfortune or other mishap. Here's how it works. Let's say Bill and Mary's total estate dwindles to $40,000. Perhaps they make a bad trip to Las Vegas or spend a great deal on problems of their children. Anyway, the law allows them to consider that they each have an estate of $20,000. If one of them is forced into a nursing home by bad physical or mental health, they must spend their assts down to $1500, which is designed to pay for their funeral. If both man and wife are facing the nursing home the spend down is $3000. Most offices in charge of Medicaid disbursement allow a spouse to place the total value of their home in their exclusion of the spend down. The spouse not facing the nursing home places the total value of the home in their name by having the other sign their share over. Notice I did not say all offices allow this. I'm not saying what I think of this law; I'm just giving you the facts. Of course, our friends Bill and Mary can avoid this problem by making their pre-arranged funeral plans pre-paid and irrevocable. Sounds pretty sensible particularly if you like Las Vegas!

My father told me a long time ago, in regard to Life Saver mints, if something only costs a nickel, there is probably a hole in it. There are a lot of life insurance salesmen, prepaid funeral salesmen, and funeral homes that will show you some pre-arranged prepaid funerals which sound miraculous. There's probably a hole in them, too. For instance, some insurance plans that are paid monthly only return the premium plus a small amount of interest if the death occurs within two years after the purchase of the policy. This leaves both the purchaser of the plan and the funeral home involved with a sack of Life Saver Mints!

Get out there and check out pre-arranged, prepaid funerals. Investigate the programs with reputable funeral firms, insurance companies and banks. Get everything in writing so that you can understand it. Ask questions and get answers. Look around. After all one of the reasons the federal government forced funeral homes to set merchandise and service price lists was so you and I can compare them. There are laws as well protecting us in our dealing with banks and insurance firms. Go for it!

Hey, it's been a blast! I've enjoyed it every minute. I hope you have learned a little about the history of my family's funeral business, something about caring for the dead over most of man's history, and had a few laughs about my experiences in both the funeral and ambulance business. Get started on pre-arrangement and pre-payment if you think it is for you. I've already started on my next book!

References

Aliranguec, Loretta M. "Funerary Practice in the Ancient Americas." Morbid Outlook, http://www.morbid outlook.com/nonfiction/articles/2003_03_americas.html.

Gies, Joseph & Frances. *Life in a Medieval City*. New York: Appollo Editions, 1973.

"Funeral Rites and Customs." Microsoft® Encarta® Online Encyclopedia 2007. http://encarta.msn.com ©1997-2005, Microsoft Corporation.

Raush, David. *Building Bridges*. Chicago: Moody Press, 1988.

"The Egyptian Pyramid." *Encyclopedia Smithsonian*. http://www.si.edu.Encyclopedia_SI/nmnh/pyramid.htm.

"Civil War Embalming." National Museum of Funeral History. http://www.nmfh.org/exhibits/holmes/index.html#.

"The History of Embalming." British Institute of Embalmers. http://www.bioe.co.uk/history.asp.

"Zoroastrian Dakmma-Nashuii Mode of Disposal of the Dead." Traditional Zoroastrianism: Tenets of the Religion. http://zoroastiranism.com/dakhma33.html.

National Funeral Directors Association web site. http://www.nfda.org/

"Mummies 101." Nova Online. http://www.pbs.org/wgbh/nova/chinamum/mummies101.html.

Ford, Tennessee Ernie. "Sixteen Tons." Capitol Records, 1955.

About the Author

Richard H. McHugh was born in October 1929, the same month in which the Great Depression began. He began his career in the funeral service-ambulance service at age fifteen. He was graduated from Indiana State University in 1951, served for two years in the U.S. Army Counter Intelligence Corps, and was then gradualted from the Indiana College of Mortuary Science in 1955. In October 2006, he received the honorary title of *Distinguished Hoosier* from the governor of Indiana.

www.ingramcontent.com/pod-product-compliance
Lightning Source LLC
Chambersburg PA
CBHW070838300326
41935CB00038B/1136